Conversation: A New Theory of Language

CONVERSATION
A New Theory of Language

Carl H. Flygt

Lindisfarne Books
2006

Lindisfarne Books
610 Main Street, Suite 1
Great Barrington, MA, 01230

The geometric figures in chapter 4 courtesy of Rudolf Steiner Press, from
Olive Whicher, *Projective Geometry: Creative Polarities in Space and Time,* 1985.

First Edition

LIBRARY OF CONGRESS CATALOGING-IN-PUBLICATION DATA

Flygt, Carl H.
    Conversation : a new theory of language / Carl H. Flygt.
        p. cm.
    Includes bibliographical references and index.
    ISBN-13: 978-1-58420-038-3
    ISBN-10: 1-58420-038-3
    1. Conversation—Religious aspects—Anthroposophy. I. Title.
BP596.I57F49 2006
302.3'46—dc22

                                                            2006003719

10 9 8 7 6 5 4 3 2 1

TABLE OF CONTENTS

For

Peng-Si Yu

and

Ou-Yang Min

for

Rudolf Steiner and the Anthroposophical Society

and for

Lavinia

to whom fate has been unkind, but whom,
for her musicality, language may yet enlighten.

FOREWORD

"WHO NEEDS A theory of conversation?" may be a reflexive response, for some, to this book. Isn't conversation as natural as speech itself, after all, if not quite so natural as breathing? For Carl Flygt, the answer is an emphatic *no*. And even a casual observer might agree to this extent: given the precipitous decline of manners and decorum through the end of the twentieth century and the beginning of the twenty-first, ordinary conversation has become more and more an anarchic affair.

Until now, conversation has resisted "formal theory," Flygt writes, because "language appeared simply to contain too much freedom for people to use it as a well-defined and objective game." Flygt draws on the work of John R. Searle to solve this problem. Searle's demonstration that users of any language "are limited to a finite number of operations" allows Flygt to apply the most rigorous reasoning of Kant to the controlled practice of conversation.

"Now rationality is the capacity to apply logic to experience," says Flygt, "and if Kant is to be believed, rationality actually makes the world what it is." But Flygt, for all he intends to develop and apply an involved set of laws, both natural and agreed upon, to what he calls "pure conversation," is not on the path of reductive rationalism. Thus he departs from Searle's belief that "human spirituality, if the term represents anything real at all, is just a systematic illusion of the brain." Flygt's new theory of conversation seeks "a material basis for consciousness," but without being, at the end of the day, a materialistic theory.

The tight focus of the theory on pure conversation is meant to develop "a tool of enormous evolutionary power," which can ultimately be applied to revision and repair of the pathology of everyday life. "Western society is currently immersed in a tidal wave of unreflective technological and material success, much of which is demoralizing and stupefying to the spiritual and holotropic impulses of the ordinary individual." Our culture now operates on the model of one vast, all-embracing Wal-Mart where inhabitants are compelled to alternate perpetually between the roles of cashier and customer, eating and excreting in an endlessly vicious circle, bound in their course by "mere chains of mechanical (albeit intelligent) causes." The larger ambition of Flygt's theory of conversation is to offer some solution to this problem.

Identity—one's sense of who and what one is—is often thought to be a linguistic construct. Flygt's theory moves this idea from the individual to the social realm. Thus "…a pure conversation is actually a reading out of a single text that shines forth, in flaming script, indifferently in the consciousness of each conversational participant. And from the principle of the text, which everyone already knows, it follows that the conversation can be one and only one string of sentences, spoken indifferently by anyone present."

If "rationality actually makes the world what it is," then a rigorously analytic theory of conversation can be the engine not only for social but for spiritual reform. Such is the radical ambition of Flygt's theory—to marshal the human intellect to grapple with the soul.

Madison Smartt Bell, 2005
Baltimore, Maryland

INTRODUCTION

None of us is as smart as all of us.
—OPEN SOURCE CODE MANTRA

A NEW THEORY OF *language?* That would be a theory of origins, and the present theory, if it is applied by the right people in the right way, may prove ultimately able to meet that very ambitious goal. But it would be more accurate to call the present essay a new *theory of language use,* a theory of how language can be used and how it ought to be used in the common society. The theory is that the whole of the human potential, which is an objective and unambiguous spiritual capacity, perhaps not always exhibited but certainly always available, is sociologically destined to be developed, refined and fixed by the correct use of language in certain formally defined circumstances. For a progressive and worldwide spiritual enlightenment in which everyone's dream life and everyone's waking life merge into something like a universal grammatical attitude and a unitary state of consciousness, language must be used in the right way in some strategic venues of culture. From there, spiritual and material effects will trickle down.

Until recently, no formal theory of human conversation has seemed possible. Language appeared simply to contain too much freedom for people to use it as a well-defined and objective game. Freedom, after all, usually confounds social solidarity. That situation changed in 1979 with the publication of John R. Searle's *A Taxonomy of Illocutionary Acts.* This was the essay that showed that users of language, any language, are limited to a finite number of operations in their actions with that language. As a consequence of Searle's analysis, language use, in its ideal application, has been shown to be rather mechanical, and if enough contextual support is available, rather transparent. It is as if we are each in possession of a social tool, namely language, that is capable of an unlimited range of possible employment, and is thus profoundly free, but that can be handled in only a small number of readily identifiable ways, and is thus in principle perfectly transparent. Searle's intellectual breakthrough puts us into a position in which, in theory at least, we are collectively in a position to observe and remediate that usage directly and in real time, and according to veridical standards, like ethereal spirits hovering with an earnest, guiding interest above and within our bodies, our emotional impulses and our self-conscious movements.

Conversation, of course, is the great medium of human experience. If conversation is ontologically profound, unambiguous and essentially meaningful, human experience may be predicted to become ontologically profound, unambiguous and essentially meaningful. If conversation is not, and I hold that in contemporary society in general it is not, then we can be certain that individual experience is not. I also hold that these features of profundity, of disambiguation and of meaning are universally valued and in basic ways constitute human self-consciousness and the human capacity to act voluntarily. It only stands to reason that if science were able gain some perspective on the phenomena of conversation, of human self-consciousness and of human freedom, and if it became able to operate on them, to engineer them and to mold them into ideal forms, society would have in its grasp a tool of enormous evolutionary power. I favor our developing this tool and taking control of this evolution.

My theory is simple, two-fold in essence, and stands as a whole to be taken up and developed by those willing and able to do so. It says on the one hand, following Searle, that everybody in a conversation *can* know exactly what was just said, and by extension exactly what the deep inner soul content of the person who said it is. It says on the other hand, on the Kantian maxim, that if the conversation is to be well-formed, everyone *must* have this knowledge. When this basic formula is put into practice, it turns out to be a very subtle affair, requiring significant intelligence, tolerance and artistry of everyone involved. It also requires perseverance and a willingness to learn. I teach this conversation theory in weekend workshops, in all its subtlety, seriousness and sublimity, with an emphasis on the social integrity and continuity of local groups. I particularly enjoy teaching in concert with others who have something of artistic substance to give to the local group, and to groups that may in turn give something ethereal to the world.

In spirit I teach Kant, who lived from 1724 to 1804 in what is now Eastern Germany. I want to know if this great philosopher's ideas about science, the world, and human consciousness are correct. These ideas say, among other important things, that the form of the world we experience, its actual geometry and its actual temporality, is the way it is because of the way our self-consciousness is as rational, formally intelligible and universalistic in both form and content. Presumably, on Kant's program, if our rationality were to change in the right way, the world itself would come to have different properties. I believe this is a testable proposition.

Kant has never been fully answered in the normal circles of academic education and discourse, which I want to address by this theory. These circles are ill-equipped to answer Kant not because they lack the capacity for formal reasoning but because they instinctively, and for good reasons, shun *occultism* and *occult knowledge*. Until the advent of my theory, occultism has seemed the least testable, least controllable and most dangerous domain of human nature and the natural world. It represents, in comfortable and responsible society, a real can of worms, full of irresponsible craziness, recursivity and narcissism, and is simply taboo. As a result, there is a terrible gap between the contents of acceptable intellectual discourse and the normative education it produces, both of which belie the validity and the reality of spiritual aspiration, and the contents of the developing human soul or astral body, which as a matter of proper development and social valuation are occult and full of mystical wonderment and intrigue. Education, if it is to lead anything really valuable out of free individuals, must lead out these occult contents.

One pioneer of modern consciousness research, which aspires to be a consensualized form of occultism, holds a similar position with respect to normal academics. When it comes to exploring the real limits on human experience, limits that are actually penetrated by time-honored techniques like shamanism and the use of psychoactive substances, many of which Stanislav Grof (b. 1941) has studied in considerable detail, the proponents of normal science, notwithstanding their respect for Kant, are most prone either to ridicule or to pathologize. But in Grof's view, and I think in the view of any honest confession of our basic humanity, the need for such experience is something he calls *holotropic*. Such experience is categorically necessary and perhaps organically instinctive in the human being—the human being simply needs to grow beyond the culture of materialist experience, and even the culture of faith and devotion, and into cosmic knowledge and cosmic wholeness. In the language of this text, the human being is an *astral spirit*, seeking to regain that status in and by means of language itself. Deny that need for intelligent and profound social experience and you sow the seeds of violence, greed and all manner of cultural and commercial vulgarity. Support it and you are apt to produce miracles.

The answer to Kant—it is clear to anyone who has experienced psychedelic drugs—is in occult knowledge. No one will think that the world *in itself* has the form we experience in the ordinary everyday. No one, for example, experiences a house simultaneously from all directions, inside as well as outside. Yet certainly that is what the house, at least in part, actually *is*. But it is plain why academic discourse, which represents intelligent discipline in the social and political use of language and linguistic products, has no use for the direct experience of the *a priori* causes of something being called "a house." These causes, should they be actualized on an ongoing basis, would overwhelm the consciousness, and its capacities would be accordingly diminished. No one, can function well in an abstract, mechanical and material society when stoned on psychedelics and confronting the ontological profundity of a thing-in-itself. A culture that indulges this experience naively, the street culture of Berkeley's Telegraph Avenue, for example, is prone to mediocrity, pathology and its own intractable forms of vulgarity and social error.

A complete and astoundingly functional answer to Kant was formulated by the Austrian philosopher, clairvoyant, and educator Rudolf Steiner (1861–1925). Other notable occultists and clairvoyants taking their departure from Kant include P. D. Ouspensky (1878–1947), whose *Tertium Organum* is a work of great genius, the English magician and mystic Aleister Crowley (1875–1947), himself a social misfit but whose protégé Israel Regardie (1907–1985) is author of a marvelous study of magic, *The Tree of Life*, and C. G. Jung (1875–1961), whose contributions to analytic and depth psychology are well-known and highly influential. The name of G. W. F. Hegel (1770–1831) should also be mentioned in this connection, whose dialectical theory of rationality is a response to Kant as much as it is to the magical histories of Christianity and the Old Testament. A basic grasp of Kant, therefore, appears to be essential to anyone attempting a rational, if not a strictly consensual (i.e. socio-political) mastery of the occult nature of the human being.

Kant's basic ontological position is *idealism*, as distinct from realism, ontological dualism or phenomenalism. Kant, like Plato before him, argued for the reality of ideas or *things in the mind*, and believed that experience or consciousness is in general a feature or a function of these things. Later in this essay I will endorse the position that these things in the mind are properly called *institutions*, and include the phenomena of language, of freedom, of truth, of social status and of spiritual experience in general. On my view, the reality of idealism is a reality devolving from a *social background of cosmic proportions* that produces a broad range of things-in-the-mind, and that thereby constitutes a broad range of possible experience.

Kant does not treat social institutions as causes of anything, but is content simply to enumerate the categories and categorical functions that have devolved somehow to rational consciousness. These include categories of *concept*, the so-called categories of the understanding, and categories of *will*, the so-called categorical imperative. His philosophy is therefore a substantially nuanced *critical idealism*, as distinct from the *dogmatic idealism* (phenomenalism) of the theologian George Berkeley (1685–1753), who denied the existence of the world except in the imagination, and the *empirical skepticism* (also a phenomenalism) of the evidentialist David Hume (1711–1776), who denied the epistemological validity of the imagination.

Kant's object was to set metaphysics, the attempt to know the true and ultimate causes of things in general, on the ground of a rigorous science. In doing this, he imagined a faculty of *pure reason*, logical thinking in the human modality but with no admixture of empirical content, and he derived his metaphysical system from that. That system denies that our intelligence, constituted as it is, is capable of knowing the true causes of appearances, the things themselves. On what that intelligence, differently organized, perhaps by means of a different social background, might reveal, Kant is silent. But *the idea of breathing life into material nature by means of well-ordered institutions* does appear in Kant's political and moral writings.

The present theory of conversation, which is politically and morally Kantian, was inspired by Marjorie Spock's beautiful anthroposophical essay, *The Art of Goethean Conversation* (1983). Miss Spock's intuition is, moreover, an explicit tribute to the work and legacy of the anthroposophist Rudolf Steiner, whose clairvoyant vision took practical shape in a large number of fields including education, medicine, architecture, agriculture, speech, drama and social science. *Anthroposophy,* meaning *wisdom of the human being,* is a term coined by the Kantian philosopher and idealist Johann Gottlieb Fichte (1762–1814), and holds in one form or another that all of the forces and dispositions of the cosmos itself are arrayed for the apparent purpose of producing human experience and the human form. On this view, human consciousness is a necessary consequence of the way the cosmos, most of which lies outside the range of the human sensorium, is put together.

Generally speaking, Steinerian anthroposophists possess all the intellectual and spiritual concepts necessary to implement my theory of conversation, and in a way the theory was written for them. But I think the theory has relevance outside explicit anthroposphical circles, and can be applied in any New Age community committed on the one hand to meditation or some systematic holotropic practice and on the other hand to some degree of social organization and communicative action. In short, my theory can and must, if I am correct in my basic assumptions, be used by *any social group trying to establish a causal link between a spiritually active life in the astral body and a cosmically harmonious and beautiful spiritual condition in the outer world.*

The current theory also aspires to the standards of logic, rigor and formal reasoning set by modern analytic philosophy, which in the catastrophic political wake of Hegel and Marx has been narrowly concerned with problems of language and mathematics, especially with the problems of linquistic meaning, logical inference, and material reference. Particularly germane is the logical materialism of John R. Searle (b. 1932), who appears intent on pushing *biologism* as far into consciousness and language as it will go. This will, I think, turn out to be very far indeed, because according to my best guess, both logical materialism and biologism are true theories. I am as committed as Searle is to discovering a material basis for consciousness and, I think it follows, for the astral body.

It needs to be recorded, however, that I find the social and aesthetic implications of Searle's textbook positions on science and consciousness abhorrent, basically because they lack encouragement and hope for the spark of individual cosmic divinity. Searle is a materialist, a positivist who thinks human spirituality, if the term represents anything real at all, is just a systematic illusion of the brain, and will be understood in terms of biological processes and ultimately the atomic theory of matter. But such an illusion, however necessary from a practical point of view, would on Searle's view lack the dignity, respect and legitimacy due either a natural or a supernatural phenomenon. Unlike lightening and thunder for example, which command the respect of everyone witnessing them because they are actual cosmic events, spiritual consciousness, including incarnation, spiritual experience and excarnation, would turn out to be a mere human construction, and contrary to all appearances and efforts to believe otherwise, not cosmic at all.

Fortunately, thanks to the structure of human freedom, it would appear to be a matter of simple preference whether we are to accept and to build a world like Searle's, which is essentially dead, earthbound and filled exclusively with mere chains of mechanical (albeit intelligent) causes, or whether we opt for an environment filled exclusively with the cosmic surprise, power and magic of spiritual causes. The present theory, if it withstands the scrutiny of contemporary culture, including the scrutiny of modern materialism, is intended to parlay that preference into an actual choice. One's choice of *conversational style*, and the company one keeps as a result, will disclose to everyone who cares to investigate which choice one has made.

The pragmatic position I hold therefore has serious institutional consequences, and great responsibility must be exercised in pursuing these consequences. Western society is currently immersed in a tidal wave of unreflective technological and material success, much of which is demoralizing and stupifying to the spiritual and holotropic impulses of the ordinary individual. The leveling of individual consciousness and aspiration through the market economy, the equalization of the sexes by means of technology and cultural politics, and the suppression of individual genius through the advent of improved methods of communication and information processing are pointing us toward a technocratic, godless and highly engineered future in which spiritual functions are adapted to lifestyle preferences, and not vice versa. I wish to hold modern institutions, and particularly our use of language, accountable for this backward and unappealing trajectory.

What Western society needs more than anything, I think, is a *meta-university.* We need to fund individuals of talent and commitment who are able clairvoyantly to study the research, the attitudes and the politics of the modern university, from which much of this unreflective success devolves, and to make insightful judgments about them. In that way, society can always remain free of the creations, television programming for example, which may threaten to deaden it or lead it to spiritually stultifying background practices, the mindset of private property for example, from which there is no easy escape. The conversational model I am proposing here, which is a model for a rigorous science of free, clairvoyant and socially adjusted individuals, can serve as the basis for the language spoken in this meta-university.

Be that as it may, the current iteration of this theory (there will undoubtedly be future iterations), in addition to its Kantian spirit, follows the philosophy of John Searle substantially in outline. From the basic theory of speech acts, to the general theory of action, to the theory of intentionality and intentional states, to mind-brain identity, to rationality and rational action, to the general theory of institutional reality, to the collective acceptance of institutional power, the theory is basically Searle's. It is intended to be a fair, if simplified restatement of Searle's commonsense and materialist views on these crucial topics. Suffice it to say that this, the first naturalistic theory of conversation ever proposed, is a Searlean-Kantian analysis of human communication, both materially and formally conceived, with the added condition, for whatever it is worth, of literal spiritual or occult enlightenment.

What is Pure Conversation Like?

Now, what is a pure conversation according to my theory? Who attends pure conversations? What do these people talk about? How many people can participate at one time? How often and where do pure conversations occur? What can we understand intuitively about pure conversation merely in reading about it and in thinking about its principles (i.e. about its necessary rules)? What can we expect to experience in a conversation framed in the way this text does?

In broad terms, anyone with a basic grasp of the principles of pure conversation and a willingness to grow spiritually can participate in them. The themes of pure conversation are best limited to predicates with well-formed ontologies, so most topics in the common world, such as national politics for example, don't work well. Topics with an *inherently high concentration of propositional truth*, such as the Buddhist Abhidharma on the other hand, are very useful substrates for pure conversation. There are many sources of such substrates from the world's traditions, and the sheer diversity and profundity of these traditions, together with *the necessity of an underlying unity among them*, will surely make for decades and centuries of fascinating, enlightening, and altogether compelling cultural and conversational work.

I have led formal conversations with groups of up to 80 individuals, but naturally the most workable numbers range from 5 to 20. The configurations in which people arrive and in which people sit are energetically significant, and represent an important study in conversation theory. Geometrical and temporal ratios of 1.618, the so-called Golden Mean, can be used in formal conversation to energetic effect, as can regular movements of individuals through space before, during and after conversation. Motionlessness is also an important capacity for conversationists to develop, and everyone participating in conversation should be capable of sitting still and remaining silent, if necessary, for significant stretches of time.

Ideally, I think, the individual should experience two well-formed conversations every day, each one lasting for between 45 and 90 minutes, or perhaps more. Such a regime should be sufficient to guarantee a lawful, healthful and lifelong growth into the higher subtle bodies. Conversations are best conducted in clean and architecturally healthy spaces, with good lighting and a minimal décor. Plants, colors and sculptural forms can be used to good effect, as can bells, flames, minerals and prisms. Alchemical techniques can be employed. Recording devices can be used if they are sufficiently unobtrusive, or if the participants are accustomed to them, as can devices that monitor physiological indicators, such as heart rate, skin resistance, blood flow and brain metabolism. Computers can be used to collate these data, and mathematical techniques employed to analyze them.

The interval between the beginning of conversation and the end is subject to objective standards. However, because of the complexity of the astral life of each conversational participant, the outcomes of this interval cannot be described, so that a reader can experience them beforehand, straightforwardly in analytic prose. Perhaps in poetry, perhaps by means of mathematics, but not by or in ordinary prose. At least not in *my* prose. Suffice it to say that human experience during a pure conversation is *otherworldly*. It is objective experience of an *etheric* world.

Notwithstanding the foregoing disclaimer, there are a couple of analogies that can help illustrate what one's experience can be like during a pure conversation. The first is the famous Sufic analogy of the blind men and the elephant. When it comes to the presence of a literal supersensible world, coincident with the world of the senses but incommensurable with it, we are all, with very few healthy exceptions, quite blind. However, if our rational intelligences are *harnessed together* through intrinsically correct formalities and mutually agreeable rules, we become collectively much more intelligent and energetic than we are individually. Under these conditions, something like a living *social organism* can come into focus. This social organism is the aim and outcome of all true conversation.

In the first instance, the contours of this organism will be *felt*. They will appear to the intuition of each individual in a private and occult way, and will prompt the individual with impulses to articulate or otherwise express some propositional content. These *conversational moments* are moments when everyone has his (her) hand on the elephant. They are full of possible meaning and profound necessity, and it is the purpose of the conversational rules to sustain, to illuminate, to explore and otherwise to work with the reality of these noumena. In this way, as an expression of our social potential, it can be hoped that an entire order of reality, heretofore unavailable to us except in dreams and in other altered states of consciousness, can be brought into full daylight and full critical cognizance. In this way the world of spirits, sorted and selected for appropriate consumption, may become an integral part of our world, of our institutions and of our common moral comportment.

The second analogy is with writing and with literacy in general. The writer takes pleasure in standing back from his (her) creation and noticing the ways in which it now appears to be imbued with *life*. If the writing is particularly good, others also notice this transcendental quality in the words and sentences. By definition, something analogous happens in pure conversation, but here the syllables, words and sentences hover in the atmosphere, like living semaphores. Life becomes a feature of the social milieu itself, and conversation a new kind of literacy. It is as though, in deep moments, the conversationists are touching one another with etheric members, interpenetrating and responding to one another in a medium filled with warm life, deep insight and compelling reality.

In the current context, a first provision for the upcoming theory needs to be articulated. It is a well-known liability of New Age communities and cultures, particularly of those relying on a strong central figure with something of spiritual substance to transmit to the world, that individuals with all sorts of emotional difficulties and deficiencies are drawn to them and tend to accrete there. Often such individuals manage to acquire social and even cultural legitimacy, and because there usually exists no mechanism for sorting them out, they manage in most cases actually to dominate the culture of the society. This almost inevitable contingency is handled on the current theory by paying attention to the following natural law:

NLIn1.0: Genius is necessary for conversation.

Not to mediocrity is conversation vouchsafed. The self-conscious sophisticate, the dilettante and the alcoholic, to name a few, are debarred by natural necessity from real conversation. Likewise the merely talented and the merely patient. What is necessary for conversation of the sort defined here is a *superabundance of energy proceeding from a hidden center of consciousness*. From this energy, if it is rightly developed, comes a capacity for spirit vision and an experience of literal ecstasy. It results moreover in an intuition that carries with it an instantaneous inspiration and an enduring uprightness. The only people capable *a priori* of conducting pure conversation are those in possession of a developed personal genius, or those aspiring to one.

Having thus raised the institutional bar to these lofty heights, it is important to explain the reasons for thinking that ordinary people can apply the upcoming principles profitably. In the first place, everyone has genius. Genius is a matter of *individuality*, and individuality is always a matter of great social interest. Celebrity status in modern society is a function of this ontological fascination with the bare existence of another personality, apparently other than oneself but somehow intimate with it. In conversation there is an almost instinctive appreciation for the manifestation of someone else's genius, provided it is basically well-formed and well-intentioned, regardless of how little or how well developed it appears to be. Pure conversation exploits this sympathetic appreciation by providing reasons to maintain it even when vicissitudes interpose themselves, and to refine it when things are going well. It is assumed, moreover, that the experience of such social good will, provided it is maintained and refined soberly and intelligently, is good for the individual and can develop just those qualities of genius that are required for conversation.

A second reason for thinking that a game that can only really be played by persons of genius can be played by ordinary but aspiring individuals is formality and the formalization of conversation *per se*. Genius has formal causes. Genius can be induced in the individual, and the current theory, which is a formal one, purports to be the method whereby this induction is best accomplished. On the theory, it is accomplished by producing an institutional arrangement, a world as it were, in which the individual is required and inspired to grow spiritually in absolute and formal terms. This second reason then is really nothing more and nothing less than the principle of formal education applied to ontological and spiritual substrates (i.e. to the soul and spirit of the human personality) and simultaneously to the original cause of society itself (i.e. to conversation). Let us acknowledge:

$CC_M EE1.0$: Principle of formal education (principle of the induction of genius).

The dependence of the current theory on moral maturity and its attendant effects, including spiritual enlightenment, clairvoyance and etheric functionality together with its social effects, including well-formed conversation, can be expressed as an algorithm, which

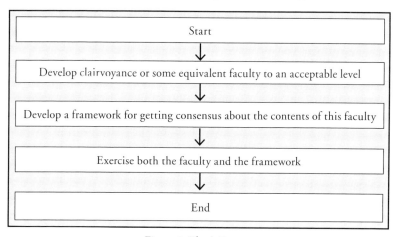

Start

↓

Develop clairvoyance or some equivalent faculty to an acceptable level

↓

Develop a framework for getting consensus about the contents of this faculty

↓

Exercise both the faculty and the framework

↓

End

Figure 1: Flygt's Program

we can call *Flygt's Program* (illustrated in Figure 1). I really don't see any way around this one, and I for one have taken it seriously.

Flygt's Program is another way of stating $CC_M EE1.0$, the principle of education. The thing is that the kind of education contemplated here is the education of a birthright. We human beings enjoy both a cosmic obligation and a cosmic birthright to become self-conscious spirits working through and floating above material nature. This obligation is individual and personal, and it is societal as well. Society should be adapted to educate the soul and spirit of the individual in cosmically lawful ways, and the individual should be personally adapted and committed to such a society. Any other form of life is basically silly. Why more people and institutions haven't taken on this program seriously and attacked this occult problem head on puzzles me. I suppose the reasons are multiple, but I suspect at their root, at least in contemporary America, they are economic.

These descriptive and sociological issues aside, and interesting and important as they may be, my purpose here is to present the *logical justification* for conversation theory. Without a blueprint for a scientific laboratory, to say nothing of building the laboratory itself, no experiments can be run. Conversation theory describes a way to set up the laboratory, the purpose of which is, following Kant, Plato and the great teachers of humanity, to set metaphysics and spiritual function in general on the secure path of a rigorous science.

Constitutive Rules: The Logical Justification for Conversation Theory

Regardless of the describability problem for the writer or theoretician of conversation, the formality condition on pure conversation requires that the principles governing it be described, enumerated and indexed. These principles are and can only be *maxims for action* adopted by the autonomous will of the conversationist. Such, at least as a first approximation, is the task of this essay. These principles in the first instance are propositions that follow *a priori* merely from the concept of conversation, or *human communication with ontological aims*. In the current text, these are called *constitutive (or transcendental) rules of conversation*, and are indexed by a numeral and the prefix

CC, signifying "conscious conversation." In the current essay, I will be satisfied to list, justify and submit for general acceptance a total of ninety-six such maxims or rules.

In addition to these transcendental maxims, which are believed to constrain (and to augment) the will and freedom of the pure conversationist, there is also a set of *natural laws* that contributes to the archetypal sculpture of conversation. These include the phenomena of genius or individuality, of sympathy and antipathy, of the etheric field or body in which human experience takes place, of the motions in this body, and of the principles of reciprocal causality between this and higher bodies and the physical body. These laws in the current text are indexed by the prefix NL, for "natural law," and here I have identified and described thirty-one. In general, the idea here is to identify all of the categorical constraints on human conversation, both natural and transcendental, and to organize them in such a way that any rational person will quite naturally accept them as the *a priori* structure of what he (she) does and must do in the presence of another such person or persons. On this basis, I think, we can hope for a self-organizing process to begin in free and affluent human societies in which spiritual causes and intelligences exercise themselves immediately on a material level.

In addition to these categorical imperatives of the autonomous will and of material nature, the text lists a number of meta-principles or rules, and a number of hypotheticals, or possible truths that can and should be subjected to empirical testing. Meta-principles are simply categorical imperatives applied to a level once removed from the maxim of actual action. Before getting started with conversational actions, for example, it is necessary to accept that conversation properly speaking has a structure. If this meta-principle is ignored or denied, proper conversation cannot begin. Such meta-principles are denoted in the present text by the prefix CC_M. As an opening gambit, therefore:

CC_MRat1.0: All conversation has a logical (describable) structure.

Hypotheticals, on the other hand, are propositions that it is not necessary for everyone to accept, but that it may become necessary to accept pending empirical justification. These should simply be intrinsically interesting to the conversationist, and will serve to elucidate the general nature and experience of pure conversation. The reader will also find in the present text's selection and organization of hypotheticals some clues to the author's ultimate theological ideas, to the extent that they exist, and will be able thereby to judge whether or not this ultimate trajectory is sympathetic to him (to her). Hypotheticals are indicated in the present text by the prefix Hyp.

Here follows some reasoning intended to illustrate how the constitutive rules are identified and to get the ball rolling. As I say above, we do not arbitrarily make these rules up. Rather, we ask what concepts are already implied by the concept we are trying to understand, and because that implicature has the force of logical necessity, we frame those concepts as rules. A concept in general is something universal that serves as a rule. The concepts that appear to be necessary to the concept under consideration, and that anyone will recognize as such, are justified and entered onto the general list of rules that constitute that concept. Further discussion and critique may collapse, eliminate or change the form of some of these rules. Many other rules beyond the ones I list here pertaining to pure conversation and to pure social experience, I am certain, will be discovered and codified by groups of individuals attempting to refine their conversational experience. Because what is being attempted here is really a lexicography of human and social experience in general, I will not be surprised if the number of such rules is found eventually to be on the order of tens of thousands.

A pure conversation is something framed in objective time. I see no other possibility if ontological satisfaction is what is desired of the experience of conversation, and *no purpose other than ontological satisfaction can possibly explain conversation in general.* People converse in order to make contact with the reality of existence. On the current theory, knowing that the conversation will have a limited life span increases its ontological value and its seriousness. It is as if knowing that a conversation is mortal builds the reality of existence explicitly into its structure. An inbuilt ontology, in turn, has an ordering effect on individual subjectivity. Thanks to a rigorous idea of time and existence, the confusion of inner impulses is brought to heel, and objective spiritual experience becomes possible. Thus,

$CC_MOM1.0$: Principle of ontological satisfaction.

Conversation in my terms therefore has a definite beginning and a definite end, usually prearranged on the clock. This *time condition* in itself is enough to set what is meant by pure conversation apart from many forms of ordinary or worldly social intercourse. Most ordinary social intercourse is governed by individual sovereignty over the inner sense, with no intersubjective time standard. In contrast, pure conversation begins under an objective temporal condition, proceeds under objective temporal and formal conditions and ends under an objective temporal condition. Let us then suggest the first constitutive (transcendental) rule of real (pure) conversation:

CCST1.0: Principle of temporal circumscription (time condition).

Almost immediately we are compelled to describe a second rule. Conversations must take place, and *must be thought of as taking place*, in some specific configuration of space. We will see that a very great deal of cosmic momentum is forced on the individual conversationist by this condition, and in a way this condition is the essence of pure conversation. It is moreover the most subtle condition imaginable, demanding cognizance of one's absolute position in space at all times during conversation. To live up to it, the individual conversationist must be prepared to join the movements of his (her) own mind with the motions taking place in three dimensional space around him (her) as well with the movements taking place in the counterspace (the extra-dimensional space) of the minds of those with whom one is conversationally engaged. For now, let us say:

CCST2.0: Principle of spatial awareness (space condition).

Now, in keeping with the spirit thus established, the first sentence of any conversation can only have the following form:

(1)   We are here to talk about p

where p is the content of the conversation. It follows merely from the definition of pure conversation that a sentence of this form must be spoken formally, and that all conversations worthy of the name contain it. Now it may be that sentence (1) is not actually spoken because everyone present already knows or thinks he (she) knows what it is, or because everyone present has agreed not to speak it, or because some shorthand version of (1) has been adopted. But these *tacit* or otherwise *degenerate forms* of (1) do not show there is no rule. They are a response to the rule itself. Thus:

> CCUniRep1.0: Principle of naming the content (principle of formal identification of the content).

Now here follows a swift series of rules that I think are entailed by our commitments thus far. Full formal justification of these rules will need to occur elsewhere, and it will be a difficult argument, but I offer them here so that the reader can have a good and early grasp of where the theory as a whole is going. I believe CCUniRep1.0 makes no sense unless it is accepted that, in real conversation, people *already know what is to be discussed*. The situation is analogous to academic protocol, in which everyone coming to class is supposed to know, by means of prior preparation, what the teacher is going to say, and is supposed to satisfy the teacher, spontaneously, if called upon to do so. In pure conversation however, there is no teacher. That function is mysteriously distributed over the whole convocation.

This *principle of prior knowledge* follows from CCUniRep1.0 in a straightforward way. In order for there to be a prior agreement about the theme of the conversation, everyone in the conversation must know what the theme is. Otherwise you won't get a pure and deep conversation, but only a degenerate form. A classification of these degenerate forms will probably prove to be a good topic for future PhD research. They range from tea time gossip and dinner time chat, to many television and radio talk shows, particularly the ones with commercial sponsorship, to decision-making processes in business, government and even science, to the message-exchange model of many academic seminars and discussions, to sexual behavior and play, to diplomacy and threats of violence, to power relations in general. Perhaps the ancient Hebrew conception of *idolatry* will prove to be useful in categorizing these common varieties of conversation.

Be that as it may, the principle of prior knowledge is a profound one and probably implicates a very large number of related principles. Of these, I will not describe many in this essay for the reason that the basic idea is pretty far out. It says that a pure conversation is actually a reading out of a single text that shines forth, in flaming script, *indifferently in the consciousness of each conversational participant.* And from the *principle of the text*, which everyone already knows, it follows that the conversation can be *one and only one string of sentences, spoken indifferently by anyone present.* Thus we have:

CCUniRep1.1: Principle of preparation and preparedness (everyone has studied, exercised and rested);

CCUniRep1.2: Principle of universal prior knowledge of the content (everyone knows what is to be shared and is, in some sense, in possession of its text);

CCUniRep1.3: Principle of indifferent expression (it doesn't matter who says what needs to be said);

CCUniRep2.0: Principle of the mystical/magical text (what is to be shared is wonderful);

CCUniRep2.1: Principle of necessary concatenation (what is to be shared is stern and sublime).

So this is how my exposition will proceed here, although I will not attempt to describe or to justify many things as deep and as difficult as the above five propositions. The current essay is a debut, and its purpose is to introduce the concept of pure conversation to individuals who may want to work with it, and I fully expect the list of rules to undergo some reworking as people of diverse background become familiar with it and begin to take it seriously. Now one way to motivate a serious appraisal of what I am describing is to show its causal relevance to the greater society. In what follows, I will explain in general how these constitutive rules function outside the enclave of conversation, and what general recourse someone has who objects to a rule, or finds he (she) cannot understand it.

Meta-Rules: The Organization of Society

All constitutive rules of conversation are themselves subject to a set of rules (their meta-rules) that follow from the concept of society. Conversations, after all, are embedded in society. The primary meta-rule is:

> CC_MSC: Only individuals who have explicitly accepted the rules generally believed to constitute pure conversations can participate in them (principle of the social contract).

In other words, pure conversations are not possible without the *explicit* acceptance of the rules which guide them. This is an old but fairly radical idea, going back to the social contract theorists of the European Enlightenment, including Thomas Hobbes (1588–1679), John Locke (1632–1704), and Jean-Jacques Rousseau (1712–1778) and to Plato (427–347 B.C.) before all of them. These thinkers imagined a state of human existence without society, but one in which the individual retained all the powers of rationality and rational action. The human being in this condition would do everything possible to maximize his own short-term advantage and to minimize his own short-term discomfort. Inevitably, it was thought, *government* would arise from this *state of nature*. The basis for the advent of a civil society, transcending the battle of each against all, was a *social contract*.

Individual human experience today and the level at which conversation is conducted in the contemporary world are both precise analogs, even archetypes, for this original state of nature. The youthful human being trying to learn meditation or any form of spiritual functionality is in a constant condition of inner stress, forever battling the organic impulses and appetites of the mind and body. Groups of individuals introduced to the concept of Goethean conversation (see Appendix A) are in a similar position, and in the absence of a workable social contract can be predicted to lapse into a war of each against all. The history of Steiner's Anthroposophical Society (1915-present) bears eloquent witness to this human liability. The emotional planes on which business, politics and ordinary family life take place likewise furnish evidence that the state of nature is still with us, ready to break out when particular evaluative circumstances materialize.

The list of rules generally believed to make conversation possible, therefore, probably represents this elusive Social Contract. What, after all is more basic to society than conversation, or ontologically motivated communication? But because conversation in its pure form has not yet risen to the level of general consciousness, or become a general background practice and capacity, individuals willing and able to conduct pure conversations are actually engaged in the process of making that Contract an explicit reality. The experience of pure conversation is in large degree, in our contemporary time and circumstance, I believe, a writing and codification of The Social Contract.

If it is more or less plain that, appearances of civilization and society aside, we each really live in a state of nature with a literal wilderness just beneath the skin, there is a second meta-rule that I think is equally crucial. It is:

> $CC_M Rat2.0$: The background principles, rules and meta-rules generally believed to underlie pure conversation are each universal and constitutive, and will be recognized as such and utilized instinctively by any rational person (*a priori* principle).

Now rationality is the capacity to apply logic to experience, and if Kant is to be believed, rationality actually makes the world what it is. So $CC_M SC$ insists that anyone interested in entering a real conversation must have conscious, intellectual or rational acquaintance with the General Social Contract, to the point of explicit acceptance or bequeathed background practice, whereas $CC_M Rat2.0$ is sure that the General Social Contract is intrinsically acceptable and necessary to any rational person, notwithstanding his (her) propensities toward xxxii • CONVERSATION: A NEW THEORY OF LANGUAGE

inner chaos. Because of these two rules, one may be certain that many a future pure conversation (and many an impure one as well!) will be devoted to talking about what a pure conversation really is, what it really is not, which rules are generally acceptable, which rules are not, and who is interpreting the rules correctly and who is not. One may also be certain that these conversations will have the aim of testing whether and how the world can be expanded simply by adopting new standards of rationality, and whether and how society can be improved simply by spiritualizing material nature.

Now there is a third meta-rule which has the force of rational necessity in conversational comportment, at least on an *ad hoc* basis. It is necessary because without it, pure conversation would threaten to stultify under an oppression of the decades of principles, rules and meta-rules that organize it, and would fail to secure the basic human need of individual self-expression. It is:

> $CC_M Tol$: Each background principle, rule and meta-rule underlying pure conversation confers rights but not strict duties on the individuals participating in the conversation (principle of tolerance or liberalism).

$CC_M Tol$ means that in the overall scheme of things, *rights precede responsibilities*. From this meta-principle, one can see a very liberal grounding for the overall theory. Of the probably tens of thousands of principles, rules and meta-rules governing genuine conversations, the *invocation* of any particular rule during a conversation is always up to the free individual. Violation of a rule does not require that someone invoke it. Conversations can always be allowed to lapse into associative, superficial and other indeterminate modes by tacit consent. The existence of a rule, however, gives any individual the right to tighten things up, and since (by $CC_M SC$) the rule is a matter of prior and explicit contract, the presence of that individual is sufficient to force the conversation back into a pure or conservative mode.

Now suppose we have achieved a basic outline of the rules of conversation and that this outline is a list such as the one appearing in Appendix B of the present text. Suppose moreover that a prospective conversationist is asked to place a check mark in one of three columns appearing adjacent to every proposition, according to his (her) Agreement With, Disagreement With, or Undecidedness About. Suppose that some positive percentage of check marks is entered in the Disagree column. What happens?

Basically we have here the beginnings of a new *class system*, and a *hierarchy of spiritual function* within the human race, much like the one that is supposed by medieval Western thought to exist in the spiritual worlds among the ranks of Angels, Archangels, Principalities, Dominions etc. Take the example of the guy (gal) who happens to feel a positive aversion to rule CCAn1.1, and explicitly refuses to abide by it. Does that mean that he (she) is banned from all society which has pure conversation as its aim? Not at all. It just means that people like him (her) fit a particular profile, and their conversations together will have a unique flavor and tone. Of course, they will not be willing or even able to abide or tolerate those who explicitly accept the rule in question, and in a sense they will occupy a lower rank in the cosmic hierarchy. But rank in the ascended spiritual hierarchies is scarcely a matter of the pride of egoism, and of the arrogance, envy and emotional abusiveness that readily stem from these facile and unpleasant human inclinations. It is more a matter of gratitude for the mere fact of an exalted existence, and a sincere willingness to confront the *self* whose inclinations and limitations have thus far not permitted one from seeing more deeply, as others have, into that existence. That at least is how the actual angels function.

Now in purely human terms the notion of hierarchical function is hardly objectionable when applied to matters of brute competence and ability. No one objects to the notion of the quarterback as against the center in an American football squad, or of the brain as against the liver in the function of a mammalian body, or of the judge as against the bailiff in small claims court. And it almost goes without saying that hierarchical functions go a long way in securing a sense of *personal identity* to those who fulfill them, be they judges, attorneys or mere sheriff deputies. But the notion of conversational function, and of the hierarchies that must manifest therefrom as a matter of necessity, suggests, to the alert critic, strains of fascism, cultism and possibly even racism. Is not freedom of speech the most sacred of all democratic rights? Are not all citizens (and all conversationists) by definition and *a priori* equal in stature, status and the right to speak whatever occurs to their minds whenever they see fit in all social circumstances? Are not all God's children equally divine?

The correct understanding of hierarchy here has to do with a precise and careful definition of the term *society*. What is a *truly social circumstance*? What is equality under *those* conditions? What is the essential difference between an explicit fascism, an explicit cultism, or an explicit racism and a tacit freedom of association that ostracizes on the basis of prejudice or impatience and ignores the duty to serve the needs of those less adept or less fortunate? I say there is none, and that only under truly social conditions, *which because they require fully self-realized actors are fully hierarchical,* can the impulses of fascism, of cultism and of racism be expected to wither away.

The conversational model that follows here clearly settles the definitions and questions about what constitutes truly social conditions. It provides both for the notion of hierarchy, which is hardly a feature of human society that can be wished away merely because people tend to exhibit arrogance and envy, and for the notion of equality, both of opportunity and of right, which is really a condition on self-realization. It provides for order and orderliness, without descending into classical fascism, classical cultism or classical racism, and it provides for individual freedom without surrendering to anarchy.

Against the charge of fascism, the following is germane. As I describe it here, pure conversation is legitimized by *absolutely democratic methods*. A single individual has the power to veto the possibility of pure conversation, and thereby to ruin the evenings of several, or perhaps dozens of other persons with a single discordant outburst. I grant that there is the possibility of a tyranny of the majority implicit here, because no sensible person wants to be thought of as a social misfit, and will instinctively tend to join with the herd. As a result of this mechanism, discordant outbursts tend to become suppressed. But democratic rule, however extreme, simply is not fascism. Conversation, as I describe it here, is not a matter of a single Lawgiver forcing a social or moral protocol on a susceptible population. It is, in essence, the willing and critical acceptance by sovereign individuals *on a recursive basis* of the fit between a set of pre-existing and somewhat malleable rules and circumstances that, as in the game of chess, appear differently each time a conversation is convoked. In this sense, pure conversation is always and only willed by a group soul of unique configuration, and must be willed anew, from first principles if necessary, each time a group of individuals convenes under the Idea of conversation.

The criticism of cultism (the tyranny of the majority) is answered by the sheer universality of pure conversation. Granted, groups of individuals may learn to function together conversationally in ways inaccessible and largely unapproachable by the uninitiated, but they are only doing what these uninitiated themselves do all the time anyway, albeit at a completely subconscious level. In a way, the world itself is a cult. People in the common world are absolutely expected not to deviate from a certain set of background abilities and presuppositions, such as walking on two legs or forming sentences from front to back, even though their alternatives may be entirely serviceable. The problem of conversation is to restore a universal form of cosmic culture, an *a priori* and cosmic cult, to the common society, which is dominated today by economics and the spiritually stultifying cult of materialism.

To anticipate the invective of racism, which is wholly unjustified by an accurate understanding of conversation theory, it needs to be said that the genius of different peoples is, well, different. But with due respect for the cultural achievements of the various races and civilizations of world history, it will be hard to deny that the white and admixed Semitic races have developed a superior politics, namely federal democracy, and that conversation theory is part of a political tradition that seems certain by right (and by might) to govern all of humanity. Or perhaps in a few centuries it will seem to be the other way around. In any event, all are encouraged to try on this particular theory of conversation. Those whom it doesn't seem to fit will have plenty to occupy them in subconscious society. Probably we will see an ultimate division of the human race – between those who want to function like angels and those who do not. But the existence of the higher functions is always predicated on the existence of the lower, whom they bend to serve. Humanity will remain unified, despite its independent evolutions.

From this model we can see a *principle of hierarchy* at work in future society resulting from an interplay of *free association* and *constitutive rules*. Of course these three factors are always at work in human society in multiple and degenerate ways. The good news is that the new hierarchy of etheric human beings will have less to do with material wealth, inherited or stolen, with material power, inherited or stolen or with a material outlook on life and consciousness in general, and more to do with spiritual capacities for art, for love and for service to others. To rise in the spiritual hierarchies, moral conduct is required, and for moral conduct to be exercised, conversation must become a moral art. Let us say:

> $CC_MHFA1.0$: Principle of hierarchical function within conversation (principle of social identity);
>
> $CC_MHFA2.0$: Principle of free association outside conversation (principle of individual identity).

Now the problem of fascism sticks a bit more obstinately to the notion, also implicit in pure conversation, of an *environmental movement of the mind*. Conversation theory is aimed, if not directly certainly in an indirect way, at all of the cultural vulgarities, emotional violations and expressions of intellectual obtuseness that inevitably come with free society. Sado-masochism, which is permissible in today's free market culture, existing for example in professional wrestling matches televised into innocent and unsuspecting private households, primarily because no compelling argument exists to promote or to legislate its alternative, cannot and will not survive the culture of pure conversation. Here, sado-masochism and its ancillaries will be treated as what they are – overly material and pathological deviancies with no desirable or useful function in the mind of the individual.

Now this rather paternalistic position on psychosomatic disorders such as sado-masochism is by no means uninformed of the legitimate and heretofore unavoidable causes of such contents in the human soul. Stanislav Grof, whose work has taken depth psychology to levels of clarity and explanation untouched by Freud or Jung, has shown quite convincingly that such contents are probably generated by strong impressions received during the birth process, which simultaneously stimulates sexual arousal and inflicts serious emotional alarm, danger and physical suffering on the infant. Nor would one wish to lay any sort of moral blame for these obnoxious contents either on the individual, who is merely victimized by powerful circumstances apparently beyond his (her) control, or on his (her) mother, who, from the meager cultural and physical instruction given to women about who and what they really are, generally remain as much a mystery to themselves as they do to their menfolk, and are consequently often in more or less the same psychological boat as the infant. It is just that human consciousness, which is often strongly and counterproductively biased by experiences surrounding birth, and which may require considerable work to outgrow them, is built for better things. We should keep in mind also that the technological fix is by no means the ultimate solution to the problem of emotional and moral maturity in the human being. Descending from an entirely artificial womb with no birth trauma whatever in one's emotional background is just as likely to produce mental and emotional patterns and contents that one will need to outgrow.

From an anthroposophical viewpoint, which is concerned above all with the right cosmic development of the human being, who and what the human being really is is something that should never have touched down on the material plane at all. The reason we are all here, and not suspended above the material plane in an ethereal world looking down on it all and intervening here according to cosmic law, is *an overwhelming desire in us to experience materiality.* The result is an almost guaranteed pathology from the beginning, resulting from the shocking realism of the birth experience. This desire for material experience, moreover, has hardly been extinguished from the average human soul merely by the fact that it has been born. We continue to pursue it in forms of freedom and power, in some cases intelligently and healthily, but in many cases unintelligently and uncleanly.

The environmental movement of the mind, to the extent that it exists today, seeks to eradicate the impure, unclean and otherwise overly material impulses and expressions of the astral body. The fascist perception here is all too facile. But what needs to be understood is that conversation theory seeks only to reinforce the higher and nobler impulses of human nature, and to allow the others simply to transform or to lapse into obsolescence. This is not fascism; rather, it is education. It is the true meaning, applied to society and culture, of Darwin's doctrine of Survival of the Fittest. Reinforce, by mutual practice, that which serves the ascent of the human being and the world to an *etheric functionality*, and allow the impulses of materialism to adapt themselves as best they can to the new environment. Thus:

$CC_MOM2.0$: Principle of emotional purification (principle of astral cleanliness);

$CC_MHFA3.0$: Principle of spiritual Darwinism (principle of the ascent of the ethereal).

Chapter 1

Basic Conversation Theory

What can I know?
How should I act?
How should the City be governed?
—The Basic Socratic Posture, 399 B.C.

"The unexamined life is not worth living." What rational mind, committed as it must be to knowledge, to justice and to happiness in itself, would dispute that claim? Is the Socratic maxim not the moral touchstone of all true conversation, and of all true society for that matter? Is there any real alternative open to those who would find truth and beauty and goodness in life, and even in all aspects of life, were they to come to believe, as a matter of objective fact, that they could?

This Apollonic ideal will give rise to the basic theory of conversation outlined in this essay. The basic theory hinges on the idea of *transparency* in all conversational and social transactions. Any social transaction that lacks transparency cannot really be said to have involved conversation; any social transaction that exhibits transparency is conversational in some sense. As we will see, the ideal of transparency goes very deep, even as far as clairvoyant insight into nature herself. Moreover, if it is pursued in the right way, it can lead us to taking up residence in a completely new and spiritually higher world, transforming us utterly as self-conscious individuals and as members of a planetary social organism. It can turn us explicitly into etheric spirits intermixed with and masters of material nature, replete with a new domain of law, of functionality and of common day-to-day experience. Let us say:

$CC_M EE2.0$: Principle of self-knowledge

The Principles of Universal Representation

The basic theory of all conversation is:

> CCUniRep3.1: Everyone participating in a conversation can
> know exactly what was just said.
> CCUniRep3.2: Everyone participating in a conversation
> should know exactly what was just said.

A conjunction of these principles, the first of which expresses the possibility of universal knowledge and the second of which expresses the necessity of such knowledge, seems to say a bit more, and can be paraphrased as:

> CCUniRep3.0: In true conversation, everyone always knows
> exactly what was just said.

It does not seem possible to argue with these ideas, or to propose an alternative. They are simply a matter of the definition of conversation, albeit a strict one. But they do have the advantage of being completely practical, as I will show below, and are readily tested for serviceability. The surprising thing is that no one in social science has insisted on them before now.

The critical predicate in these definitions is "know exactly." I will not attempt a full and formal justification of this idea here, because it is a difficult one, but I think its basic sense is "to possess." If someone knows something exactly, is master of something, he (she) in some sense has possession of it. Now this is a deep idea, because on these definitions of conversation, it is necessary for someone to know or be in possession not only of the formal syntax of the current conversational content, but also of the *motivation* behind it. Granted that A said "xyz;" *why* did he (she) say it? Only if everyone is satisfied that they understand this and assent to the expression of its token in the moment do we have the basic condition of conversation.

The foregoing condition, of course, hinges largely on $CC_M OM1.0$, the principle of ontological satisfaction. In pure conversation, we are always satisfied by the self-presentation of others. More precisely, we are always satisfied that we understand the self-presentation of others. It is by no means necessary to be sympathetic with that self-presentation. It is only necessary that we be satisfied with how we assess that self-presentation.

Now such a condition could scarcely be codified, much less enforced as a rule, if it were not *a priori* apparent that the sole motive of conversation is *ontological satisfaction*. This is both a matter of stipulation in the current theory and a matter of empirical fact discoverable in general use. Our language in form if not always in self-conscious usage is preponderantly composed of ontological claims. This is because all uses of the predicate "is," whether explicit or implicit, are sufficient to determine that status, regardless of how well or how poorly, how sincerely or how insincerely, how forcefully or how weakly that claim is made. An ontological claim or an ontological impulse is always subject to conditions of satisfaction, and conditions of satisfaction always have an explicit content, code or conceptual rule. The mere presence of an explicit content, code or rule, moreover, necessarily implicates the presence of a well-formed motive. More on this in the section on judgments below, and in the chapter on intentionality (Chapter 7).

It is easy to see the gulf that opens up between ordinary subconscious conversation in the world, and pure or conscious conversation. It does not do in the practice of business, of politics, of science or of society, high or low, to require a full disclosure of the motives of those one is dealing with. One must make do with character inferences and character judgments. But the conditions are different in archetypal conversation. Here, motives and background dispositions are understood as clearly as propositions, and these motives, at least when judgments are involved, are always ontological. Thus we have the critical corollary:

CCUniRep4.1: Principle of transparent motive (principle of contextual insensitivity).

One conversational consequence of universal, exact and ontologically satisfying knowledge is worth rehearsing at this juncture, having to do with attitude. The Platonic dialogs, which in many ways are the model for the present theory, are predicated on the set of questions appearing at the outset of this chapter. These idealistic and self-searching questions really do get to the heart of real conversation, and they cannot be over-invoked. In preparing for conversation, the expectant anticipation of which is as vital as its actual execution, the individual is mindful of his (her) spiritual strengths and weaknesses, particularly with respect to the text (CCUniRep2.0) of the upcoming exchange, of his (her) relations with others and of his (her) grasp of the procedures governing the upcoming exchange. The knowledge and background disposition one possesses or professes to possess, of oneself, of objects and of complex relations in large part actually is who one is. Real conversation and real society is a transparent disclosure of that condition to all others, to oneself and to the transcendental omniscient spirit traditionally called "God." In real conversation, we stand spiritually and ontologically naked, amid ideal and objective forces in the cosmos itself. Thus,

> CCUniRep4.0: Principle of ontological nakedness (self-consciousness condition);
> CCUniRep4.2: Principle of idealistic motivation (principle of idealism).

The presumed normativity of this confessional approach to social activity, if not its potential for moments of acute self-consciousness and embarrassment, is likely to concern scientifically-minded readers, who want their theories not only to be universally valid, but also to accord with the Prime Directive not to alter the phenomena they purport to study. The reply here is that the present theory accounts for *all conversation*, ideal as well as degenerate, and captures the essence of all conversational action, which *in itself* is normative because it is idealistically motivated. The theory is not normative but descriptive. It describes a system or world phenomenon, namely self-conscious human communication, which, if the term can be applied meaningfully to a universal motivation, is itself normative.

Now idealism in general is an appeal to what is best in ourselves, in nature and in the products of our activity. It is the stance that always looks for improvement, for an elevation of standards and for refinement in what we experience and what we express. It is a principle manifestly at work in our institutions and in our social order, at least in those progressive social orders of the West. All academic standards with the grading marks from A to F, all enlistment by government and business of the "best and the brightest," all optimism, wealth accumulation and powerful social myths like the American Dream are direct reflections of the social power and the institutional reality of idealism. Conversation theory is an attempt to recast idealism into a new form that can make nature herself respond to the sublime spiritual potential in the human mind.

Notwithstanding the disarming and revolutionary import of the basic transparency principles, CCUniRep4.0 and CCUniRep4.1, and of the idealism contained therein, let us turn our attention to the precursors, CCUniRep3.1 and CCUniRep3.2, which will be of greater interest to the scientific reader. Both of these propositions are derived from categorical analyses. The first, CCUniRep3.1, derives from John Searle's taxonomy of illocutionary actions, which says there are five and only five things a speaker can do with language, and consequently that a certain amount of objectivity is built into our language use, whether we choose to be serious about it or not. Searle's taxonomy has been neither refuted nor questioned since it was first suggested in 1979.

The second, CCUniRep3.2, derives from Kant's analysis in 1785 of what constitutes a good will. Kant's idea is that a good will, which is certainly basic to human communication and human comportment in general, can be nothing but a *law of nature*. This is the famous categorical imperative, the critical (philosophical) justification of moral law. Here Kant describes something that looks a lot like the universal moral admonition to "Do unto others what you would have them do unto you," but that Kant claims is derivable from the logical notion of *all* or *every*, together with the idea of autonomy, the giving to oneself of a concept or rule that determines one's action, or even one's thought impulses. I will further explain Kant's categorical imperative later in this chapter.

Searle's proposal is that there are a finite number of things someone *can do* when he (she) uses language. This *finiteness condition* on language and language use makes conversation theory possible, because without such a condition it would be unthinkable to insist that a *universally identical representation* (e.g. CCUniRep3.0) of some conversational content (and even of some conversational motive) is possible. Now it is true that Searle's taxonomy only provides the possibility of absolute agreement on the *form* of some propositional or meaningful content (see below), but the possibility of an absolute (categorical) starting point is crucial. Once such agreement is accomplished, it is only a matter of applying a good will to get agreement on the *substance* of what was just said.

Principles of Expressibility and Causal Reference

At this juncture, two very important concepts from the philosophy of language need introduction, the *principle of expressibility* and the *theory of causal reference*. The first has the force of general acceptability in philosophy, at least in representationalist circles, and says that anything that can be meant by a speaker or would-be speaker can be expressed in language. On this principle, *intentions contain language*. The mere impulse to say or do something is already a linguistic (a rational) event. In a sense, conversation theory is really about the *impulses* to speak and to understand. In this sense, pure conversation occurs entirely on this pre-articulate level, before any actual speech takes place.

The second, due to the logician Saul Kripke (b. 1940), has its philosophical opponents, but is so generally plausible and ontologically significant that it borders on being a principle. It says that any act of linguistic reference, whether naming someone or something, forming a proposition about some entity or just thinking about him, her or it bears a literal *causal relationship* to that actual person or thing. That causal relationship is usually very obscure to trace, should one wish to attempt it, but it must exist.

If I speak of "Caesar," for example, the picture (or feeling) that is evoked in your mind has traveled there, through space and through time, from an actual moment in the scnse world when the *person of Julius* (or Augustus, depending on which Caesar is meant) was *formally coupled with the term* "Caesar." The situation is similar to the old vinyl impressions of sound recordings. On these, when one listens to Led Zeppelin's unnamed album (1971), for example, one is listening to *Jimmy Page himself* running those majestic, soaring riffs on *Stairway to Heaven*, or those brilliant and powerful syncopations on *Rock and Roll*. On the causal theory of reference, the possibility of all reference works this way. The images in the mind literally reach back with causal feelers to things and events in the world (including events in the imagination) which at some point were given the name they now possess.

One can readily see the relevance of this picture of linguistic reference to a theory of conversation that requires that everyone present have identical knowledge of what everyone else is thinking. In a truly *social* situation, such as a pure conversation, what is of utmost importance is that nobody be left behind. Everybody, if the event is to be a social one, properly speaking, must remain in direct contact with the objects, entities, and situations that are being talked about. For this reason, it is best in conversation not to pile up too many abstractions. If someone says something abstract, for example "If Christianity had not occurred, television would not have been invented," it will almost certainly take the rest of the evening for everyone to feel comfortable with the idea, if not with the speaker. After all, by CCUniRep4.1, the speaker's motives need to be sorted out. The worst thing that could occur, from the standpoint of telepathic conversation, is for someone quickly to rejoin, "If we had had television when Christ walked the earth, Christianity would never have occurred."

Thus we have:

NLSem1.0: Finiteness condition (Searlean taxonomy)
CCExCR1.0: Principle of expressibility (principle of the conversational impulse);

CCExCR2.0: Principle of causal reference (principle of material efficiency).

A Guiding Taxonomy

Now, let us turn to the basic taxonomy of the conversational use of language. It is important that all conversationists listen for this basic structure in all expressions of conversational content. Doing so will make the logic of conversational actions universally transparent and will make it possible to avoid many conversational wrong turns and social impasses. It will, moreover, make it possible almost immediately to begin studying the motivations and actual self-nature of those gathered for conversation, which is what the game is really about. The possible forms of speech and interpretation (understanding) are:

Assert or judge (p)
Direct someone else (p)
Commit oneself (p)
Express (p)
Make a declaration (p)

where p is the content (i.e. the substance) of one's speech (and, by the principle of expressibility, of one's soul, mind or action) and asserting, directing, committing etc. are psychological attitudes, modes or states that one can adopt in the moment.

Judgments: In the first case, an assertion or judgment is a state of mind with a content such as:

(1) Snow is white.

By CCExCR2.0, the principle of causal reference, if someone asserts (1) conversationally, a natural phenomenon actually occurs in the room. The configurations of the speaker's (and the interpreter's) brain, like a section of weather, is momentarily constituted by snow and by whiteness, i.e. by *what the speaker (interpreter) synthetically remembers* of "snow" and *what the speaker (interpreter) synthetically remembers* by "white." On the theory, judgments, which are always truth claims, must, like weather patterns, be accorded considerable circumspection, even reverence. They are claims on reality, and not just claims on some individual's reality. They are claims on other people's reality, on universal reality and on the reality of the conversation itself. Let us say:

CCJ1.0: Principle of the judgment (principle of assertion);
CCJ1.1: Principle of judgmental circumspection (principle of reality invocation).

It should also be understood clearly that *all locutions of the form*

(2) A is B

are judgments or assertions. The unthinking New Age admonition *not to make judgments* (which of course invokes Christ's command at the Sermon on the Mount: "Judge not that ye be not judged,") is fatally undermined by the fact that all uses of the predicate "to be" are judgments. Christ had special plans for his early audiences, and gave them the unique discipline of appearing in public without any expression of intellect ("Let your speech be yea, yea: no, no: and that which is over and above these is of evil." Matthew 5:37). It is quite impossible to function conversationally without intellect, and in that sense we can never be pure Christians. But we can know very clearly when a judgment is being made in our presence, and even what ultimate ontological significance that judgment has or intends for us or for others. If we take on the Principles of Universal Representation systematically, we can come up with something that Christ may yet approve.

Directives: Continuing with Searle's taxonomy, the general form Direct someone else (p) is satisfied by locutions such as:

(3) Please pass the salt; and
(4) Present your weapon, soldier!

These *directives* are best understood in general as *requests*, whereby the speaker specifies an action to be carried out by an interpreter or hearer at some time in the future. In general *questions* have this form, because every question asked is a direction to provide some kind of information. Thus the question:

(5) Where is your sister tonight?

is logically parsed, on the current theory, by:

(6) I request (you tell me right now (location of your sister tonight)).

The conversational significance of directives is profound because they explicitly close off certain semantic possibilities and explicitly open other, usually very distinct possibilities. Directives are treated in the current text in the next two sections of this Chapter, as well as in the section on Meaning in Chapter 7. For now, suffice it to say that directives, and only directives, move conversation along. They are the engine of conversation, and are embedded in the deep structure of nearly every conversational speech act. Let us say:

CCDir1.0: Principle of the directive.

Commissives: The general form Commit oneself (p) is satisfied, for example, by the following locutions:

(7) I'll be at your place by 7:00 p.m.; and
(8) I promise to pay this bill.

Here the speaker commits himself (herself) to a future action.

The purely conversational significance of commissives is hardly more limited than that of directives, but in a different way. Although conversation based exclusively on commissives would be semantically rather limited, it might be very satisfying (see Figure 2).

Commissives play a tremendously important extra-conversational role in the decision to accept the numerous logical and political

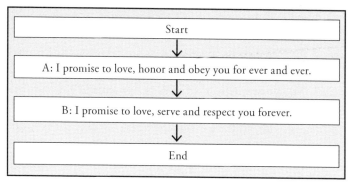

Figure 2: A Purely Commissive Conversation

conditions on pure conversation, as well as practical ones such as the time and place of a specific meeting. The significance of commissives is in the role they play in deontology and collective intentionality. Every conversational judgment entails a commitment by the speaker to the truth, sincerity and evidence of his (her) action, and all of the other classes of conversational action entail analogous commitments. Moreover, by the principle of expressibility, we say, on the present theory, that these commitments are as good as spoken. It is as if, in saying, for example:

(9) Socrates was bald,

one simultaneously says,

(10) I promise to withdraw this claim (Socrates was bald) if someone shows it to be false, and
(11) I promise to furnish evidence if somehow required to do so (Socrates was bald), and
(12) I promise redress if someone is injured in relying on this claim (Socrates was bald).

In short, a commitment to *authority* or *deontic power* is what comes with every conversational action, and a commitment to authority is in large part a construction of an *originator* or a *self.* When we find ourselves able to commit to some linguistic entailment or set of entailments, and actually do so, we enforce, modify or even make anew the spiritual ego (the spiritual originator) we each require to function intelligently in material nature. Likewise autonomy, the Kantian principle of the moral will, is nothing more and nothing less than the free origination of rules or concepts of action to which one commits oneself in the manner of a formal promise.

Similarly with collective commitments. When we collectively accept that so and so has the power to do such and such, we collectively create a social bond or a social unity (a social institution). In future epochs, this institutional bond may prove to have a function as intimate and essential to us as that of the spiritual ego in our own time, but distributed socially over individuals. The possibility of a *social organism*, the basic ontological aim and objective of all conversation, is to be derived from the commitments we make in our speech and in our thoughts by accepting the causal power (the authority) of a world of contents that descends directly out of the cosmic spaces and intelligences of actual spiritual beings. True social solidarity is cosmo-mechanical. In this sense, and contrary to contemporary appearances, institutional power and causal power are actually the same concept. Let us say:

CCCED1.0: Principle of the commissive.

Expressives: The general form Express (p) is satisfied by:

(13) Ouch!

and, if spoken (and interpreted) in the right way, by

(14) Oh that this too, too solid flesh would melt!

These *expressives* have the sole function of expressing the psychological state of the speaker, and are not to be confused with *judgments about* psychological states, possible or actual. For example, the locution

(15) I wish my flesh would melt

is not an expressive, but a judgment, and is logically parsed by:

(16) Judge (I am a person who wishes his flesh would melt).

Expressives used effectively in conversation would indicate the achievement of a high form of art. It might be possible, for example, to hold a conversation in which various sentiments and impulses were expressed solely by reciting, either from memory or by means of some sort of artificial access, applicable passages from literature and poetry. The metaphorical plane thus achieved might be richer by far than anything mere individuals could conjure on the spur of the moment from their limited and freewheeling imaginations. Highly refined applications of such techniques could lead to genuine social telepathy, with its attendant wonder and amazement. Let us say:

CCCED2.0: Principle of the expressive.

Declarations: Finally, locutions of the form, Make a declaration (p) are satisfied by sentences such as:

(17) Class is dismissed; and
(18) War is hereby declared.

Such speech acts have the effect of altering the real structure of the world. It is a remarkable fact that the bare utterance of a declaration, if the institutional facts in which it is embedded are right, can causally affect the world of nature, the material world of atoms, molecules, conscious states and macroscopic objects that constitute the reality we know. Let us say:

CCCED3.0: Principle of the declaration.

The Conversational Directive

People in conversation of course incline toward a complex and often subtle usage of these five categories. Sometimes an individual can express something subtle in a way that is completely transparent, but most often subtle usage leads to *conversational implicature*, generally an expression of egotism. Such implicature, unless immediately identified and purified, is fatal to conversation in the strict sense. Conversational implicature was described and given a theoretical treatment by H. Paul Grice (1913–1988), a fine English philosopher and semanticist during his tenure at the University of California at Berkeley.

On the current theory much conversational implicature is a consequence of the *propositional structure of meaning.* Whenever someone says something propositional and means it, he (she) is *proposing something actionable* to his (her) interpreter. He (she) is giving a *conversational directive.* Because the most common mode of speech act is judgment, the most common form of the conversational directive is:

(19) Direct (interpreter accept as true (p))

Suppose someone says:

(20) George W. Bush, after September 11, 2001, had no choice but to invade Afghanistan.

In this case it is suggested by implicature, on Grice's maxim of quality, that the speaker will be understood as saying:

(21) Direct (interpreter accept as true (history has a design of its own)).

Now it may be quite impossible for everyone present to respond to (20) in the way required by pure conversation, i.e. by accepting the truth of "history has a design of its own." Actually, not many people today believe this proposition, and a great deal of procedural sophistication would be needed to deal with (20) effectively in a pure conversation. If this were not accomplished, and as far as a pure exchange of mental contents is concerned, (20) would be likely to function as a *conversation stopper.* Let us say:

NLSem2.0: Law of conversational implicature.

Now NLSem2.0 does not mean that conversational implicature cannot be used in pure conversation. It just means that the stakes are raised somewhat when it is. As a matter of fact, conversational implicature can be used liberally and to considerable artistic effect if all the participants are intellectually sophisticated or perhaps telepathic. But for the sake of pure conversation, we do well not to allow the implicatures of a conversational interlude to pile up or go unanalyzed. Pure conversation takes place under a *universalized directive*. Unless the precise sense of the conversational directive, each time it is introduced, is understood and explicitly accepted by everyone participating in the conversation, the propositional status of any and all subsequent utterances in the conversation is subject to individual interpretation and individual action. This is the common pattern of most conversation encountered in the world today, and in that case, conversation in the pure sense remains a remote and vain hope. Therefore, we have:

CCDir1.1: Principle of universal direction.

The Universal Directive

Now what is the attitude necessary to conform to CCDir1.1, the principle of universal direction? This turns out to be Kant's *categorical imperative* in its most sublime and its most spiritual variant. Pure conversation is *pure social activity*. In it, the ego is severely curtailed and sublimated in its expression, and the will, which the ego necessarily directs, takes a form which is sensitive to the *social consciousness* (the rational human experience) of everyone present.

Kant's analysis gives several presumably equivalent dispositions of a good will:

1. The good will is a *law of nature*, where nature is a harmonious and organic whole;
2. The good will entails *respect for any and all other wills*;
3. The good will acts in harmony with the idea that *other wills are creating universal laws*.

4. The good will creates universal law as a member of a *realm of intentions.*

Kant's picture, if it is to be taken seriously, can only represent the human potential as intrinsically angelic, for what can 1–4 above describe but an abode of angels? If this is what actually stands behind all settled and prosperous society, and certainly if anything does it is the good will, what can be done to make our conversations represent it even more explicitly? Why is our world still so imperfect? Why does it still cry out for justice, for freedom and for unqualified solidarity?

Kant's ideas about the good will come from a careful reading of Jean-Jacques Rousseau, whose theories of human nature and the social contract were instrumental not only in the French Revolution of 1789, which momentarily overturned the callous and self-indulgent rule of the French aristocracy dating back to the Feudal Ages, but also in the mind of Karl Marx (1818–1883), who produced a theory of society without private property. Rousseau believed that human nature, although instinctively prepared for self-defense, is essentially compassionate, generously and humanely wishing the best in others and ready and willing to assist those less fortunate or less capable. It is only because we have left the state of nature and opted for possessory society that we have lost the birthright and capacity to function as the angels do, with a kind and earnest regard for others in all manner of circumstance.

To be sure, according to Rousseau, we have fallen quite a way in our capacity for possible experience. Our natural and sensitive impulses are corrupted and suppressed by a society rent with commercialism, avarice and warlike inhumanity, by relationships and institutions that defy and defile the benign natural languages spoken by the heart. Our experience is not ecstasy but mutual isolation and alienation; we experience and think of ourselves as separate beings in the abstract company of other overly powerful, merely manipulable, completely untouchable or otherwise inconsequential beings. Power relations dominate all. At the sight of a suffering man, we avert our eyes and say, "He is no business of mine."

For modern man, his fellow man can be killed with impunity underneath his very window. He has merely to place his hands over his ears and argue with himself a little in order to prevent the nature which rebels in him and cries out to identify himself with the man being assassinated and tortured. (*Discourse on Inequality*)

New York City perfectly represents the object of Rousseau's critique, from the 1964 murder of Katherine Genovese under the windows of thirty-eight respectable and law-abiding citizens in Queens, whom she knew and who for more than thirty anguished minutes refused to offer aid of any kind to the dying woman, to the 2001 spectacle of the World Trade Center burning and collapsing to the ground. After this latter event, people in New York and in America did begin to be measurably nicer to one another, and somewhat broader in attitude, a marked change from the economic boom years of 1996-2000, when the Enron corporation, for example, was at its apogee. But one does well to ask why it took such a heavy-handed demonstration to accomplish the change, if fundamental change it was. Perhaps Osama bin Laden's satirical and even artistic critique of American culture and of American capitalism will someday rank with that of Rousseau, although it will not be able to claim the same caliber of motive or of intellect.

What to do? Something basic needs adjustment in our society, and I think I know what it is. The institution to reform is not private property, as Rousseau thought, and not government, as Bin Laden apparently wishes, but everyday language use. The faculty to educate is not the intellectual so much as the aesthetic. In a sense, we must learn to stand against intelligence. We must find ourselves able to look at the intelligence of materialism and of capitalism from a viewpoint of moral intelligence, spiritual reality and a humanly scaled economic power. If we do this, we will gradually find it possible to transform the society that fundamentally alienates us into one that uplifts us wholly.

The passage from the old society to the civil state must produce a remarkable change in man. It must substitute justice

for mere instinct in behavior and give his actions a moral quality that they previously lacked. Only then, when the voice of
duty and responsibility replaces physical impulse and right replaces appetite does man who had hitherto taken only himself
into account find himself *forced to act on other principles.* If
we can do this, our faculties will be exercised and developed,
our ideas will be broadened, our feelings will be ennobled.
Our entire soul will be elevated to such a height that we might
seek constantly to bless the happy moment that pulled us away
from our previous society, that transformed us from stupid,
limited, narrow and selfish people into intelligent beings and
men. (*The Social Contract*)

The *general will* is Rousseau's term for the ecstatic moral consciousness that he presumes will be able to govern and administer
not only the sensitive social experience of naturally constituted human beings, but also the surpluses of economic activity accruing to
such society. The general will is simply what everybody wants from
life—a deep unity of consciousness permeated by profound truth and
organic health—made subject to rational policy, decision and law. It
is public responsibility, the moral values that define a society at its
best, and the freedom or empowerment to act out of a habit of care
and goodness. It was this difficult concept that stimulated Kant to
formulate in remarkably precise philosophical language the analytic
concept of the good will.

Harmoniousness and respect between and among the wills of
men and women is the essence of Kant's moral law. It is law accepted
willingly. Without these, conversation in the strict sense is not possible. Most conversation we encounter in the world today is a shell, a
shadow of the possibility of pure conversation. In it there is little that
moves the soul and less of cosmic momentum and of cosmic import.
Under the direct action of moral law, by way of an almost unimagin-
ably glorious contrast, our intrinsic freedom shines forth from the
body in supernal light and color, and men and women move like
deities through a living world in the passion and moral force of their
own originary impulses. Thus,

CCDir1.2: The general will (what everybody wants, rationalized);
NLM: The categorical imperative (the moral law).

Chapter 2
THE META-CONVERSATION

When we think we're using language, our language is using us.
—DEBORAH TANNEN

THE GREAT SOCIOBIOLOGICAL QUESTION is how causally relevant the world of dreams, spirit vision and personal enlightenment, which is the aim of all pure conversation, is to the world of institutions, machines and massive objects in high gravitational fields. Can, for example, a group of people enjoying the ecstasy of a well-formed conversation make good practical decisions affecting the administration of a governmental body or of a reserve of capital? Will spiritually adept individuals organized socially prove to be more wise or less wise in dealing with practical and material reality? Was kingly initiation a sound social practice, with possible relevance to a liberal democratic society, or is it too much to ask of clairvoyant wisdom to play an administrative role in our technocratic future? The current theory gives us a way to test these questions.

To that end, the concept of the meta-conversation must be understood. All consciousness is supervened by a *transcendental unity*, and the consciousness possessed by the social organism is to be no exception. The governing intelligence of any conversation is always a second conversation with a more limited scope of reference. This meta-conversation is a continual sorting, selecting and invoking of a set of rules and expectations that may apply, should anything less than perfect satisfaction obtain, to the current expression or the current content. The meta-conversation is formal agreement (formal unity) both about what just happened and about what happens next. Ideally, it proceeds by reference to a well-formed and indexed list of rules that everyone has already accepted and internalized, and is ready to call up should things begin to spiral out of control.

Readers familiar with formal semantics and the semantic theory of truth developed by Alfred Tarski (1901–1985) and his followers may be concerned to establish a connection between the meta-conversation defined here and the meta-language, usually involving set theory, that Tarski used to make a strict definition of truth in certain limited languages possible. Surely our semantic notions (the laws or rules by which we appeal to truth) are what really control our conversations, and if the meta-conversation is what is responsible for the control of pure conversation, perhaps the meta-conversation will follow the lead of some formal semantics and ultimately be reduced to it.

The fly in this ointment, however, is that a Tarski-style meta-language contains more predicates than the object language it is designed to describe, whereas the meta-conversation defined here contains fewer predicates than the conversation it is supposed to control. At the same time, the current theory proposes an altogether new and non-Tarskian semantics, a semantics indexed to a spiritual text floating somewhere in the cosmos that predates and under certain conditions explicitly predetermines everything that we do, think or say. It also proposes a significantly expanded notion of truth, outlined here in Chapter 4. Let it suffice to say that an incorporation of formal model-theoretic semantics into the current theory of conversation has yet to be accomplished.

The Meta-Position and Self-Regulation

Individuals familiar with *neurolinguistic programming* (NLP) will recognize the practical feasibility of carrying on two conversations alternately in two different *states of consciousness*. As NLP shows, there is always a *meta-position,* an actual altered state of consciousness close to an out-of-body experience, available to anyone engaged in self-conscious rational activity. In pure conversation this witness position is *strengthened to the point of pre-eminence.* In pure conversation, at ideal and essential moments, everyone is actually functioning, quite rationally, outside the body, or better, is functionally embedded in a greater spiritual body. This suprapersonal function is caused by the *purely formal requirements* imposed on conversation by the meta-position and its laws. The situation is strictly analogous to one's performance in yogic meditation or tai chi. One's experience under these conditions is exalted the more faithfully one conforms to the instructions and careful monitoring of the experienced teacher. In conversation, the difference is that, as in the realm of the angels, everyone is the teacher.

Meditation, then, which is the paradigmatic meta-attitude, is the real principle of all conversation. One practices meditation with and only with reference to instruction on how to stay self-conscious. I am proposing in this essay to describe the basic set of instructions that anyone interested in pure or self-conscious conversation will affirm as necessary and assert when needed if such conversation is to be attempted at all. Let us say:

$CC_M Rat3.0$: Principle of the meta-conversation (formality condition);

$CC_M OM3.0$: Principle of meditation (principle of the meta-attitude).

These meta-principles of attitude and conversation are related to another set of basic ideas, the principles of regulation, or autonomic response. No conversation can survive unless each individual is willing and able to regulate the manifestation of his (her) own impulses to meet a certain baseline of tacit acceptance, and over and beyond this to submit, at least in principle, to the regulation of these manifestations by the judgments and directives of others. It may be demonstrable that much of this regulation has objective correlations, in the manner of universal biofeedback. I do not actually find it farfetched to imagine a group of out-of-body conversationists all wired for the gamut of physiological measures and being given signals from a central computer about who is currently positioned where in a multidimensional psychobiological space. The laws maintaining or constituting this space can only be laws of self-regulation or autonomy.

The strong version of the principles of regulation says something else, namely that each individual is subject to the acceptance and satisfaction of everyone in the conversation. This "everyone" *includes the person himself (herself)*. The strong version of conversational regulation thus entails not only a universal input into the matrix of conversation, and of its lawful causes, but also universal self-knowledge. Everyone in real conversation must be contributing a positive quantity of well-ordered (i.e. universally acceptable) energy and attention. Everyone in conversation, moreover, must be settled within himself (herself). In addition to being positively engaged, everyone in transcendental conversation must be self-realized, because self-realization is a necessary condition on the capacity to let go and to function outside the body. Let us say:

> CCEng1.0: Principle of engagement (principle of participation);
> CCSR1.0: Principle of self-regulation (principle of autonomy);
> CCJ1.1.1.1: Principle of external regulation (principle of heteronomy);
> CCSR1.3: Principle of self-knowledge (principle of self-consciousness);
> CCUniRep3.3: Principle of testing.

Legal Considerations and the Principle of Non Sequitur

Tracking and verifying the legitimate reference of all speech in conversation is a basic function of the meta-conversation. The meta-conversation is a conversation about the current form of the conversation. If the substance of the current conversation is not always a straightforward matter of universal agreement, the substance of the meta-conversation always is, or at least should be. The meta-conversation, by definition, is always a matter of universal agreement. Without it, moreover, no conversation of any kind is taking place.

The meta-conversation is thus a continual updating of the *legal status* of the conversation. In ordinary discourse, this updating is left largely to tacit background practices. On my theory, the meta-conversation needs to be conducted explicitly, at the same time as the substantial conversation. Once all participants have the hang of things, and are comfortable with a high level of conversational function, the meta-conversation can be allowed to relapse into tacit modes. These reformed modes, however, will inevitably be at a much more refined level of energy and attention than was otherwise possible.

In actual practice, it is not unusual for this meta-conversation to occupy much or even most of the time and attention available for a conversation. This is because there are probably thousands of universal rules that constitute conversation, many of them still undiscovered and unarticulated. Naturally, it does not always prove possible to get immediate agreement on which rules to apply at a particular conversational juncture. Patience, tolerance and stamina, as well as imagination and a good memory, then become vitally important in the practice of pure conversation.

Another way of putting the principle of the meta-conversation is to say that pure conversation is a matter of the rights and duties conferred by the set of *status functions* generally believed to legitimize conversation in a particular context. These status functions (which are another way of naming the constitutive rules I am attempting to list here) are testers or indicators which when invoked return a positive value ("yes" or "no") in deciding whether or not the current expression should be given conversational status. The meta-conversation is a sorting of these functions or rules to determine their application to the current conversational moment. For example, suppose someone (A) says:

(1) We are here to discuss Aleister Crowley's theory of magic.

and someone else (B) says in response:

(2) Solid lithium combines with nitrogen gas to yield lithium nitride.

Unless everyone present senses the causal reciprocity between the contents of (1) and (2), a meta-conversation is immediately invoked. The rules governing the exchange must be clarified, and the exchange itself must be declared legitimate or illegitimate. Is there a logical link between (1) and (2)? If so, what is it? If not, is B being deliberately provocative? If so, to what end? Is B sincere? If

not, is B mentally ill? If yes, can B be remediated? If yes, is reme-
diation inside or outside the scope of the present conversation? If
outside, is the present conversation finished? What, in short, is the
status of the conversation, now that (2) has occurred? The process
of responding to such questions is the meta-conversation.

To put the foregoing point a little differently, we say that a conversation is always and only about some *content*, p. If a logical or contextual non-sequitur occurs, and you suddenly find yourself talking
about something else, say q, you are not really having a conversation.
You are really trying to have two conversations, or more probably,
you are just drifting along together in a subconscious manner with
no intention to hold a conversation at all. Let us say:

CCNS1.0: Principle of non-sequitur

Ontological Principles

Now the meta-conversation, and the lawfully ordered altered states
of consciousness that can be produced pursuant to its logical and legal
requirements, depends heavily on the following proposition:

$CC_M OM1.1$: All conversational impulses are ontological.

In other words, everyone with linguistic or rational consciousness
in conversation is actually trying to come to terms with the reality
of existence. The meta-conversation, the meta-attitude, the witness
position and all spiritual impulses generally speaking are motivated
by the human need to do *fundamental ontology*. That is simply what
everyone is doing all the time with their rational energy and attention, and it is what really produces society. No social theory can, I
think, do without this notion.

With this grand proposal, the basic theory is completed. In conversation, everyone can always know exactly what was just said, everyone ought always to know exactly what was just said, and everyone is always trying to harmonize himself (herself) with the reality
of existence. Where no impulse can be detected either to sense the

precise content of the conversation or to sense the reality of existence, no conversation is taking place.

Consider for example two teenage girls chatting about boys, clothes and an upcoming vacation. A Searlean analysis of their speech will infallibly detect an inordinate number of ontological claims, probably at least as many as the sentences being uttered, and perhaps more. For example:

(3) Bill is really cute.
(4) The shoes I bought yesterday are too tight.
(5) Next month should be, like, awesome.

Each of these sentences makes reference to some state of existence or being, and represents an attempt to place the inner reality of the soul in direct contact with an external reality in the world. Each of these sentences is a judgment or an assertion, a speech function that returns a *truth value* and thereby a proprietary claim on the reality of existence.

It is almost impossible to imagine a conversation that makes no ontological claims. Even the most silly, stereotyped and banal exchanges perform this function. Certainly the serious ones do. On my theory, ontological claims are a basic human and social need, and are directly connected with the nature of human experience and language.

Now, in ordinary discourse, ontological claims about the world usually entail ontological claims about the speaker as well. This fact stems from the *structure and function of the imagination*, and it is important for conversationists to have some basic grasp of it. A very precise analysis of this *double ontological reference* is found in the transcendental deduction of Kant's *Critique of Pure Reason*, and this analysis is certainly a worthwhile study if one has the inclination, time and guidance. Kant, one recalls, was concerned to refute both the position of Berkeley, who held that the imagination contains everything of real existence, and the position of Hume, who thought the imagination contains nothing of real existence. On this topic, in place of Kant's abstract *epistemic critique*, relying as it does on the transcendental self which formulates judgments about appearances, I offer the following, an analysis of the possible contents of the imagination.

In the first place, some contents of the imagination are mainly subjective. They are essential mainly to the self nature (the personality) of the person who projects or experiences them. For example sentence (3), assuming it is uttered in the normal teenage manner of trivial excitement, would refer mainly to how the speaker experiences Bill, to her own inner feelings and sensations, not to who or what Bill actually is.

In the second place, certain contents of the imagination appear, at least on occasion, to disclose an *actual reality* to the person experiencing them. These appear to be suprapersonal objective realities, and completely to transcend the habits and inclinations of the personality. Examples of these contents include experiences in meditation and in spiritual dreams. Such experiences, to be sure, are rare enough for most of us, but they do occur unmistakably.

In the third place, there are imaginative contents that appear to *coincide with the sense world*. Possible examples of these are physical practices, such as athletics or traditional medicine, where concentrated mental focus plays a role in physiological performance. An Olympic high jumper may be taught to visualize specific contents for the sake of improved performance. A Chinese physician may look at the flow of *chi* in the body of his (her) patient and take remedial action, usually with good results.

The best example of imaginative contents coinciding with and in some sense constituting the sense world is *magic*, or applied synchronicity, which despite its general lack of moral sophistication, is the oldest social tradition in human history. In certain cases, magical effects in the sense world are probably actualities. Nature after all would be both inconsistent and completely imponderable if there were *never* real coincidences between mental contents and objective realities.

Thus we have three types of imaginative (and conversational) contents:

A. Contents with no ontological reality outside the subjectivity of the speaker or interpreter.
B. Contents that disclose a purely spiritual reality, with no apparent relation to the sense world.
C. Contents that disclose a reality that appears to coincide with the sense world.

With this in mind, the above sentences (3–5), which for the most part are about sensations and feelings, and therefore cannot represent serious attempts to coincide with sense reality, and certainly do not rise to the level of pure spiritual experience, should be understood conversationally as:

(6) I like Bill.
(7) The shoes I bought yesterday are too tight, and I am displeased about this fact.
(8) The vacation next month should be awesome for me.

This reinterpretation of sentences (1-3) is the sort of thing that takes place in much ordinary conversation, particularly in conversation where connotation and intension are in free play. If A says,

(9) George W. Bush is ruining this country

B may wonder with justification,

(10) In saying that and in that manner, who does A take himself to be?

Much of the entertainment value of ordinary social discourse resides in just such ontological directives, and their attendant emotional titillation, and people who are skilled at exploiting these generally rise in society. The mere prostitution and exploitation of the transcendental self, however, is hardly something that pure conversation can countenance. The point of pure conversation is to draw the transcendental self out of its exploitative and self-indulgent hiding places and into the light of semantic rationality and socialized spiritual activity.

In general then, ordinary conversational judgments have a double reference, both to things in the world and to subjective feelings, sensations, inclinations, preferences and biases. This double ontological reference needs to be specified and actually purified for conversation to be conducted at a high level. In the best possible case, all self-reference implicit in conversational contents is eliminated, and speech refers only to objective entities. Our girls then might clean up their speech a little by using the following sentences instead of the ones that please them:

(11) Bill is beautiful and good in his way;
(12) Those shoes are too small for these feet;
(13) The idea of next month's vacation would excite anyone in my position.

Let us say:

$CC_MOM1.2$: Principle of double ontological reference.

Laws of Self-Defense and Satisfaction

Now we have seen that ontological judgment, ontological reference and ontological need are the fundamental motivators of conversation, and that these are reasonably construed to constitute a basic feature of the meta-conversation. However, at a more instinctive level, the human being is also motivated to defend his (her) comfort and sense of well-being (his (her) sense of self), often to the detriment of all but a semblance of external society. The human being thus desires fundamentally to enjoy reality or existence, but only in a way that preserves an acceptable standard of individual comfort and apparent well-being. Thus:

NLPsy1.0: Law of self-defense (law of comfort).

Most communicative intentions are intentions to invoke, convey or otherwise sense the reality of existence. Insuring that this intentionality is accomplished as well as possible, given the law-like limitations of comfort and self-defense, is a basic function of the meta-conversation.

The principle of comfort is not the end of the conversational story, however, because what is typically sought in conversation is actually more profound and more erotic. Conversations are centered around ontological *satisfaction*. Satisfaction has acute cognitive and spiritual elements that go beyond the mere sense of safety and comfort. These elements involve *centers of energy* in the human being, including the focusing and circulation of subtle energies both inside and outside the physical body. These energies in turn are features of the variegated tissues of the body (or perhaps it is the other way around) – the blood and nerves, the bones and joints, the soft and hollow organs. In the end, either the individual is ontologically (energetically) satisfied by the current status of the conversation, or is dissatisfied. The signal of satisfaction or dissatisfaction is the outward sign of the meta-conversation. Thus:

NLPsy2.0: Law of satisfaction (law of the cosmic centers).

It may seem peculiar to assert that the sense of satisfaction or dissatisfaction is the ultimate content of the meta-conversation. Satisfaction and dissatisfaction in themselves, after all, at least on the face of it, have no linguistic content whatsoever. They consist only in grunts, grimaces and profounder ontological states. But this meta- or para-linguistic feature of our consciousness and experience, our sensations and feelings of satisfaction and its opposite, is precisely what can link our conversations and our ontology to cosmic law itself. Ultimately, we exist in order to be used, materially, by the cosmos, and not the other way around. Ultimately, we exist in order to give cosmic law to the astral and etheric worlds, and thereby to this world. Ultimately, the tender sentient state of the individual soul is the cause and motive of all action, of all speech and of all social comportment in the domain of cosmic law.

Physical Law

Ultimately the meta-conversation must be a matter of *physical law*. Ontological satisfaction is energetic satisfaction (Chapter 6), free human actions are causally determined (Chapter 5) and the proprioceptive self-sense, which is responsible for keeping the human body upright and generally self-conscious, is produced in the brain as a probable matter of physical law, between the afferent stimuli of the sense organs and the efferent impulses of motor control. The meta-conversation, when implemented in real time, exploits just these laws of human consciousness and human experience. Pure conversation, I believe we will discover, is ultimately controlled by nothing more and nothing less than physical law. Thus,

HypPhy1.0: Hypothesis on physical law.

Physical law in general is a matter of *geometrical* or *spatial intuition*, and an exact statement of any real law of nature appeals to just these spatial intuitions. Newton, who believed in the absolute and *a priori* status of space, wrote out all his physical proofs in a geometrical form. Even after Einstein, everyone recognizes that the law of gravity (the inverse square law) is a consequence of how gravitational field strength varies in proportion to spatial area in a plane. Similarly, the law that water be identical in all possible worlds with H_2O is a consequence of the *shape of the water molecule*, as electrically polar and physically asymmetrical. Geometrical intuition, of course, is a consequence of space itself, the external (objective) condition on all consciousness, rationality and aesthetic experience.

The meta-conversation is an actual appeal to physical law. It is a search, through and by means of a well-ordered society, for the etheric and cosmic reality supervening on all linguistic impulses and all linguistic expressions. As a self-conscious and universal intervention in the physical spaces and counterspaces subtended by the living body, it is both an appeal to and an invocation of natural law in itself. It is an intention to maintain spatial appearances as a *particular type of world* (a particular state of affairs) devolving from an ordered domain of self-conscious, physical and essentially moral causes. These are the causes issuing from the mere *presence* or *state of being* of a physical human body applying a well-formed will to ideal mental contents in the presence of other such bodies. Thus:

CC$_M$OM4.0: Principle of physical law as such (principle of spatial manifestation).

Positivism is the paradigm which dominates not only contemporary attitudes toward nature and natural law, but also, somewhat unfortunately, our attitudes toward one another. For positivism, a natural law is simply a functional or a causal relation, never an *a priori* moral, social or spatial condition on experience. It is an abstract and largely deadened composition of relations, properties and magnitudes in the world which, if we understand them, we become free to make use of as we see fit and as we are able. It is also an attitude which is nothing short of disastrous for our spiritual potential.

An *a priori* physical or natural law really is something ideal and sublime. It is something which, were our existence or the existence of a consciousness relevantly like ours absent from the scene, would not otherwise exist. It is moreover something before which we quite naturally bend in respect and reverence, and to which we always seek to conform in attitude, thought and deed. It is the karmic power and the glory of universal order, and the standard by which all our attitudes and actions are ultimately judged, in life and after death. It is what confers dignity on the self-conscious human being, and makes of him (of her) something like a terrestrial star within a spacious firmament of other terrestrial stars. It is this aspect of natural law that I wish to identify with the meta-conversation.

The virtue of positivism, of course, is that it makes the excesses of idealism virtually impossible. The self-conscious human being is all too ready to appropriate for himself (for herself) the features, real or imagined, of being a terrestrial star, and of attempting to impose that glamor on others. The ego is all too inclined to collapse into the fantasy of self-importance and grandiosity, of irresponsible illusionism, of magical thought and magical thinking. But positivism makes uncritical and expansive magic look merely ridiculous. The sun does not circle the earth but is a small star at the periphery of a small cosmic galaxy, life is not a vitalistic essence but a mechanical feature of the DNA molecule and consciousness is probably no sort of *res cogitans*, but a functional feature of the brain. Positivism, which in certain guises is fully endorsed by the current theory, makes us intellectually and socially responsible, but at the same time, spiritually dull.

For classical positivism, which is still largely with us in contemporary academics and science, consciousness has *no spatial features at all*. I doubt, however, that any real positivist has ever slowed down his (her) stream of mental associations enough to take a completely satisfying breath. If he (she) found it possible to do so, s(he) would immediately discover that bodily consciousness is filled with spatial features, and that the abstract apologies of positivism for its lack of metaphysical closure represent nothing more than egotistical resistance to the spiritual and spatial necessities of a natural and *a priori* condition on bodily self-consciousness. Those necessities, in a word, are spatial laws of the cosmos in its higher etheric and astral dimensions. They are the laws of the coherent dream world, of the idealistic actor and of the free and self-realized human being. They are the laws of mysticism and enlightenment, of magic and clairvoyant vision, of the breath and luminosity of angelic beings in their commerce with the moral thoughts and impulses of the human mind.

The meta-conversation, far from necessitating the ancient *yoga of breath*, which is an outdated and socially questionable approach to the entire spiritual domain, requires of us a *yoga of light*, a top-down and social approach to spiritual consciousness. The meta-conversation focuses not on the bloodstream and the spatial energetics of the diaphragm and spinal column, although an acquaintance with these cannot hurt, but rather on the *impulse to judge*, on the impulse to achieve ontological, bodily and ultimately spatial satisfaction through language and the functions of language. The meta-conversation is what makes us and our self-expression into a law of nature. Let us say,

$CC_M OM5.0$: The yoga of light.

The law of cosmic centers (NLPsy2.0) is what links physical law, the only possible claim to scientific respectability, to moral law, the rules governing human conduct in well-formed conversation. The great law of physics, of course, is the conservation of energy. Given any dynamic physical system, the energy at work there cannot disappear. It can only change shape. The cosmic centers are the modalities in the human energy system (the human consciousness) into which energy can and by natural law actually does flow and transform, and in general these are focused in the soft organs of the body, in the heart, the brain, the liver, the lungs, etc. In conversation, these centers and their laws are plainly functional, but they are subsumed under an autonomous law that is willed in addition by the personality.

One can immediately see the physical problem of accounting for the transformation of energy in an individual human system, to say nothing of its patterns in conversation. To predict the motion of a many-bodied star cluster is beyond the ability of our physics, and this system is relevantly governed by only one form of energy, namely gravity. How apparently impossible to account physically (spatially) for the motions of energy in a system of cosmic centers which not only contain a fairly large number of "bodies," or energy sinks and energy sources, but where the form of energy itself is not well-defined, and may be multifarious. This double perplexity of many centers and undefined energy may be at the root of the so-called "explanatory gap" in the neurobiology of consciousness, the apparent impossibility of getting a reduction of subjective states and qualia to the spatial structure of their microscopic correlates (i.e. to the neurons and their harmonic resonances) in the way that the essence of water is very well explained by the shape of the H_2O molecule.

Notwithstanding these daunting problems, it appears nevertheless perfectly feasible to apply the conservation of energy not only to the problem of consciousness on an individual scale, but also to the same problem on a social scale. Human energy is certainly conserved, but it is very slippery. Sometimes, to be sure, it is plain which organ (which center) is calling the tune. When a Chinese boxer accurately squats, kicks and spins with no forethought and with an inner stillness in his motion, the center in the navel, and no other, is the transformer of the energy. At other times, however, the energy of consciousness seems to disappear into an occult modality, with no availability to the personality. At still other times it appears superficial, excited and largely useless. But whatever the particular case, and even when the energy is apparently lost to consciousness, one may be reasonably certain, whether in meditation or in conversation, that the energy in consciousness is conserved. Thus:

> NLPhy1.0: The conservation of energy (the great physical law).

Building on this, things begin to look a little more tractable to the physicist of consciousness when the principle of the meta-conversation is introduced. The meta-conversation is the principle of self-regulation and self-control writ large. It is the principle of universally acceptable dispositions (causes) of energy, attention and language. It is the principle by which our conversations and our social life in general become direct exponents of natural law. This meta-conversation simplifies the problem of consciousness considerably, because under it, although we may not know the specific form of the energy we are playing with in conversational consciousness (calories? ergs? electron volts?) at least *we can all know it is there*. Because of the meta-conversation, we can all, as a very practical matter, unambiguously sense the energies of consciousness, and presumably, with enough practice, make exact and universal judgments about them. Thus:

> $CC_M OM6.0$: Principle of universally acceptable causes (principle of the common cause);
> $CC_M Rat4.0$: Principle of intuitive unity (principle of disambiguation).

Metaphysical Necessity

Notwithstanding its respect for and in some sense its commitment to positivism, the meta-conversation represents a kind of *conceptual* or *metaphysical necessity* in the dispositions of self-conscious energy and conversation. Metaphysical necessity is the sort of thing imposed on our thinking by Newton's proof of the law of gravity, or by Watson and Crick's discovery of the structure of the DNA molecule. Now that we have those concepts, and although they might conceivably have been different in this world or in others, there is a metaphysical and ontological onus on us to cleave to them as representations of how things actually are. They fit everything else we know too well to be taken as arbitrary. They have the effect of binding together everything we know and both making it coherent and making it open to further discovery. This unifying and open-ended character in general is the effect on us of the discovery of a natural law, and in general is what is meant by something universally true being metaphysically necessary.

The present theory then, which is nothing more and nothing less than the meta-conversation in propositional form, aspires to just this metaphysical necessity. Ultimately, like physical law itself, and like the meta-conversation in its over-arching social function, I believe this theory of conversation will be shown to have a supremely geometrical or spatial form. The angels are lines and figures in space, and these angels live and move in our rational and moral thoughts and impulses, which likewise must be lines and figures in space. This theory, if I am right about it, will explain or make fit together all of human experience, actual or possible, because all human experience is essentially moral and rational. By metaphysical necessity, it will deliver us, as a socially intricate, magical and super-spatial jigsaw puzzle, from the mediocrity and tyranny of the average everyday, and catapult us into a domain of luminous and spiritual society and consciousness. It will force us to be free. It will create out of our social consciousness a world of endless happiness and satisfaction, of profound and sublime judgment and of unqualified and free instruction, reciprocal support and individualistic love of the deed. It will make it impossible for us to think of ourselves as and to be anything other than divine cosmic entities. Thus,

$CC_M OM7.0$: Principle of metaphysical necessity

The Principle of "As If"

The philosopher Hans Vaihinger (1852–1933) developed Kant's ideas about the rational unknowability of the reality of existence in a pragmatic direction. In order to survive, Vaihinger thought, man must construct fictional explanations of phenomena "as if " there were rational grounds for believing that such phenomena are realities. Logical contradictions between what we accept about the world and what we understand about it are simply disregarded. Thus in physics, man must proceed "as if " a material world exists independently of perceiving subjects; in behavior, he must act "as if " ethical certainty were possible; in religion, he must believe "as if " there were a God.

Vaihinger thought our irrational acceptance of phenomena and of categorically pure ethical judgments was justified because there exists no rational solution to the problem of understanding what these things really are. Conversation theory takes a different tack. Ultimately, we don't want rational solutions; ultimately, we want ontological satisfaction. We can accept a considerable amount of mystery in the world as long as we feel ourselves to be growing into it. Ontological satisfaction is not a matter of being able to tell others how things are; ontological satisfaction is a matter of participating with others in how things are, and allowing the mystery of existence to emerge always before us.

For conversation theory, which is both pragmatic and Kantian, the philosophy of as-if is somewhat reversed over Vaihinger's version. In conversation, we act as if we were angels, although none of us really understand that mystery. Most likely, the actual angels don't understand it either. They just act as if they do. Therefore,

CC$_M$OM8.0: Principle of as-if (principle of the acceptance of mystery).

Chapter 3

LOGIC

1. Be informative
2. Be truthful
3. Be relevant
4. Be clear
—H. P. GRICE, *Logic and Conversation,* 1975

LOGIC IS THE backbone of rationality, and is the fundamental deontic requirement on anyone aspiring to self-conscious conversation. Every soul has its logic; every conversational impulse can be made logically intelligible. The trick of truly rational (and truly social) conversation is to make it absolutely necessary for the logic of the moment to be transparent to everyone. Let us say:

> CCLog1.0: Principle of logic;
> CCLog1.1: Principle of logical intelligibility.

The principle of logic says that all conversational content and all conversational expression is subject to the standards of logic. The standards of logic are notably simple and are outside no one's ability to grasp in general terms. They are in essence the meanings of the following concepts:

> and
> or
> not
> if . . . then
> all
> some
> possibly
> necessarily

Modern logic can be traced largely to the efforts of the mathematician Gottlob Frege (1848–1925), himself a Kantian philosopher, to produce a script, one might even say a language, that would interpret itself to any logical mind. What more could one want out of a language? The *notation and ideal of modern logic*, which owes its genesis to Frege's *Begriffschrift* ("concept script") can have a very salutary effect on efforts at pure conversation, which aspires to its own form of self-interpretation. Translating the current conversational content into even a simple first-order logical form can do wonders for the universality requirements on pure conversation.

The ideal of modern logic is proof. In the same way that Euclid's theorems are shown to be necessarily valid in the way they are argued from first principles, sentences in language can be shown to be necessarily valid if they are well-formed and follow from rules governing their constituents. The effect of this proof principle on spiritual conversation is immediate and all-pervading. Under these conditions, everyone is quietly forming proofs of their utterances in advance of offering them for consumption. Call this:

CCLog1.2: Principle of logical notation;
CCLog1.3: Principle of logical proof.

To illustrate CCLog1.2, the principle of notation, consider the following sentence of English:

(1) The king of France is bald.

The first order translation of this sentence, which is due to the philosopher and mathematician Bertrand Russell (1872–1970), is:

(2) $\exists x(Kx \wedge \forall y(Ky \rightarrow y = x) \wedge Bx)$

Some qualified individuals consider (2) to be the greatest sentence in philosophy. Perhaps it is, and here is the reason. It is absolutely impossible not to slow down and *think* when something like (2) is thrown at you, and seriously claimed not only to have an intelligible meaning, but actually to capture the meaning of its natural language analog (i.e. (1)) with unexceptionable precision. On the theory of first order logic, it will be impossible for anyone to misunderstand the meaning (the references) of (2), provided he (she) thinks about it long and hard enough. For conversation, both in theory and in practice, the benefits that accrue from slowing down the thought process and actually *willing* it are legion and cannot be overstated.

Here is how to interpret (2). $\exists$ is called the *existential* quantifier, and is read "there is some" or "there exists." $\forall$ is called the *universal quantifier*, and is read "for all" or "for every." Both B and K (and for that matter, both $\exists$ and $\forall$ as well) are called *predicates*, and are understood to describe properties of something. In this case, B represents the property "bald," and K represents the property "king of France." Outside any first order sentence, both x and y are called *free variables*, and can represent anything whatsoever; inside the sentence and governed by the quantifiers, they are called *bound variables*, because here they have a specific reference determined by the attached predicates. The $\rightarrow$ sign means "if ... then" and $\wedge$ means "and."

So, (2) is read:

(3) There is some actual x such that x is a king of France; and furthermore, for any y whatsoever, living or dead, real or imaginary, past, present or future, if y is a king of France, then y is identical with x; and furthermore, x is bald.

This may appear to be a rather incredible way of asserting that the king of France is bald, but logicians agree that it is correct. The rigmarole in the middle of both (2) and (3) is to find an unambiguous way to express the concept of denotation, the concept that points to the unique king of France, the concept "the."

It may seem daunting to face the possibility that such a high level of abstract logic in principle is required of everyone in pure conversation. But how else can universal agreement about what was just said, whatever it was, be adjudicated on a final and incontrovertible basis? How else can we begin to expect even a modicum of universality, if not actual *Turing universality* (i.e. bivalent programmability), out of our social situations and our inner cosmic thought life? Pure conversation requires an absolute extensionality of all the terms used to make reference during the conversation, and by CCExCR1.0, the principle of expressibility, an absolute extensionality of the minds (souls) participating in it. Pure conversation is a transparent medium. Opacity of reference is simply ruled out.

The principle of extensionality has important consequences for the mood of conversation. Everyone in pure conversation is transparent to everyone else. There are no individuative intensional states, or if there are, they occur within tolerable limits. In a sense, in pure conversation, there is no right or principle of privacy, there are no individual evaluations. Pure conversation is a social affair. Under highly social conditions, and in the manner of an intelligent dream, the boundaries of the self are sensed from a purely logical and sometimes from a preterlogical point of view.

Things lighten up considerably when it is understood that in a pure conversation, everyone, by definition, understands what was just said. Suppose during a conversation it becomes necessary to effect a translation like (3). Either everyone will understand this translation, or not everyone will. If not everyone (call him (her) Q) can follow what is being said, everyone else must adjust his (her) tempo, alter his (her) conversational expectations, or otherwise sacrifice his (her) personal agenda and bring the conversation to a level that Q can accept. This may make it impossible, for example, to get to the bottom of the meaning of the word "the," or to take another example, to reach a decision about what to do with the $100,000 windfall that just accrued to the school's trading account. But these things might, and perhaps even should, pale in importance when set against the value of saving a soul who is lost, confused or otherwise estranged from the social body.

In general then, the principle of logic says that, for the sake of universal transparency, all contents expressed in conversation are translated into first order logic. Each conversationist makes this translation inwardly, and when necessary the content is spelled out for the sake of public agreement. This requirement alone goes many leagues toward eliminating the many varieties of me-talk commonly experienced in the conversations of our post-Freudian era. It also slows down the associative machinery of the undisciplined imagination, and opens it to public scrutiny. Logic, in short, is the great unifier, and in its higher and more sublime applications, becomes the *logos*, the spirit of truth.

Now not all contents (thoughts) can be expressed readily in first order logic, and sometimes different first order translations of the same content appear to be possible. Not to worry. From the principle of tolerance (CC_MTol), we have the *option*, not the requirement, in pure conversation to insist on strict logical form. If someone says something that falls into either of the above two categories, the group *as a whole* may either (1) momentarily relax the standard of strict logic and thereby the standard of pure conversation, and allow the expression to stand; (2) nullify, negate or otherwise take back the expression as though it had never occurred, thereby resetting the conversation to the stage of the previous context; or (3) work with the expression until it can be represented logically to everyone's satisfaction. This latter option is best accomplished by means of the crucial technique of *reproduction*.

The Principle of Reproduction

Conversational reproduction is the essence of moral law. It is the intention to reproduce the causal reality of the speaker. It is an unqualified gift of energy and attention to the ontological reality that in that conversational moment expressed itself through that individual. It is the effort to will as that person has willed. When everyone does this for the sake of someone else, that someone else senses himself (herself) as recognized and regarded in a way that, with the exception of the experience of naive love, simply transcends the possibilities of the sense world.

Neurolinguistic programming has a technique in which, in order to gain access to the subject's state of consciousness, the investigator literally exchanges positions with the subject. This is the spirit of conversational reproduction; when we reproduce what someone just said, we really do try, like actors, to reproduce that person. This can be taken as far as reproducing the tone of voice, the posture, and the characterological features of the person we were not previously able to understand. That is one approach. The other approach is through logic. Try to capture the essence of what was just said in something as close as possible to a formal sentence in first order logic, so that that person (and everyone else) can hear it reflected back, and can recognize it living in the mind of someone else (and of all others).

If the cause of the speaker's state of consciousness, regardless of how well or how poorly it was originally expressed, can be rekindled to everyone's satisfaction, a *unitary state of consciousness* appears to be the necessary consequence. Under these conditions, everyone present is subject to the same causal influences, and in theory at least, everyone will be in the same state of consciousness. This will need to be verified with measurements, but it is reasonable to suppose that under such conditions, everyone present will have the *same mental content*. Under these conditions, and only under these conditions, can the conversation admit a further ontological judgment, and so work its way to a necessary conclusion. Thus we have:

CCMn1.2.1: Principle of indifferent reproducibility;
HypPsy1.0: Hypothesis on identical mental content.

The Fundamental Algorithm

It should not be surprising, then, that pure conversation has a programmatic algorithm. What else could be expected of a protocol that requires *transparency of reference* (extensionality) of everything said and of everyone saying it? Here is that algorithm in an easy-to-understand form (Figure 3). The conversation begins. Someone makes the first utterance, and it is a meaningful one. Everyone is perfectly satisfied by what he (she) just heard. Someone, anyone, makes the second utterance, and again everyone feels perfectly satisfied. The third content is uttered. This time, however, someone doesn't like what he (she) just heard. He (she) wants to oppose it, negate it or change it. But by the rules of conversation, *all he (she) can do is reproduce it*. Inevitably however, by the principle of double ontological reference, $CC_MOM1.2$, and despite his (her) best efforts to reproduce the content faithfully, his (her) own agenda will creep in to what he (she) says and how he (she) says it. Content number 3 will begin

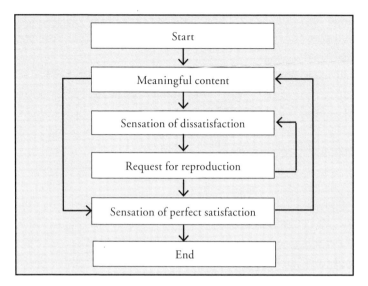

Figure 3: The Fundamental Conversational Algorithm

to transform and take on a life of its own. Call the current content content number 3_1.

Now, either everyone is satisfied with content number 3_1, or not everyone is. If not everyone is, someone will offer content 3_2. At this point, everyone is working very hard to establish just what content number 3 really is. A certain amount of tension will seem to hang in the atmosphere. Real spiritual efforts will be underway. Blood will be stirring, and the etheric body rotating. People may even be sweating. Under these conditions, someone will eventually say something that everyone can relax about and accept. Everyone will affirm perfect satisfaction with content number 3, even if that satisfaction is only nominally perfect. By definition, everyone will feel very good inside.

Now, however, the real work begins. Someone must articulate content number 4. A minute or two of silence may be necessary at this juncture, or perhaps not. Ideally, content number 4 will come simultaneously to the surface in the mind of everyone present. Someone will venture to express it. Let's say this time that everyone senses it to be the correct content, and that nothing more needs to be said.

The conversation is over and everyone departs in silence, bearing a seed from the flower that just laboriously unfolded in the etheric body.

None of this is to say that honest differences of opinion and viewpoint cannot arise in pure conversation. They can. As a matter of fact, conversations are most interesting and lively when individuals manage to oppose one another psychologically but maintain good conversational form. Under such conditions, the spiritual individual is disclosed in sharp outline to everyone present. Under these conditions, conversation becomes *high art*.

On the other hand, one ultimate presupposition behind conversation theory is that *everyone can reach agreement on everything (on anything)*. Every soul has its logic, every point of view can be deduced from universally acceptable premises. Given enough opportunity and enough good will, serious opposition between personalities must dissolve in mutual understanding and acceptance. In the end, if enough care is taken to put oneself in the other person's shoes, all difference and separation between personalities can be transcended. Let us say:

CCMRat3.2: Principle of mutual interpretability (principle of necessary validity).
CCLog2.0: Principle of extensionality
CCLog2.1: Basic conversational algorithm

God's Program

The overarching idea here is that, more likely than not, real conversations are subroutines in a system of *cosmic logic*. Call this preterlogic God's Program. What God's Program does, or is supposed to do, can be inferred, to an extent, from the nature of pure conversation itself. God's Program must be to spiritualize planet earth. It is meant to transform the human being into an order in the cosmic hierarchies, into an angel or something like an angel. It is to make human life on earth a transcendental affair of life, consciousness, emotional satisfaction and material mastery. In that process, it is to transform material nature into a new form of living material spirituality. Thus we have:

HypSoc2.0: Theory of God's Program

I refer again here to the phenomenon of intelligent or spiritual dreams, which if not furnishing direct evidence for the existence of God's Program, at least make the hypothesis plausible under charitable interpretations. There are two things to notice about these compelling experiences, which as I have said are rare enough but are nevertheless something that all of us have experienced. First, they sometimes exhibit an intelligence that is simply classes beyond the sort of intelligence we are accustomed to experience in the ordinary everyday. Where in the world could such intelligence come from? Second, they sometimes reveal a certain futile recursivity in the activities among the denizens of the dream world. It is as though these beings, exalted and sublime though they are, are likewise stuck in certain routines much like the repetition of our own day to day existence. Perhaps these hyperintelligent and sublime beings, the beings we meet in these dreams and, if we are adept, in waking visions, benefit from our presence in their world just as we benefit from their presence in ours. Perhaps we can be of help to one another in breaking out of our mutual cycles of recursion. Perhaps we are supposed to. This seems to me as good a theory as any.

Undoubtedly the theory of God's Program will be opposed by materialist/positivist philosophers and others who see no compelling *natural cause* for the institution of pure conversation. There are two answers here. On the one hand, to accept the notion of pure conversation it is not necessary to affirm all of its principles, but only some critical subset, and the theory of God's Program does not seem particularly critical. On the other hand, we may someday find it necessary to revise our conception of nature to include logic, preterlogic and *a priori* causes in general. If this latter necessity is suggested by experiment, then God's Program will simply become part of our social background, and the objections of today's materialist will seem merely quaint and outdated.

The Laws of Antipathy and Free Association

Now, in addition to the crucial notion of reproduction, the basic algorithm depends on the notion of *ontological satisfaction*. Satisfaction is the principle of the ego. It has its analogs in hunger, thirst, elimination, breath, exercise, sleep, sexual desire, worship, absolution, labor and artistic expression and appreciation. Ontological satisfaction motivates spiritual seeking. Ontological satisfaction, the highest, most erotic form of egoic motivation, is what the human being needs in order to have good dreams at night.

It is a facile matter, perhaps automatic, to sense dissatisfaction in the self-presentation of another ego. Particularly under the conditions of formal conversation, the presence of another fills the soul with antipathy. Under such conditions, unless adequate meta-programming has been instituted, it is impossible to imagine a *social* situation arising. As soon as someone says something in a conversation, everyone is on guard. Some will want to attack the speaker, some will want to defend themselves, and no one will want to let the expression stand, unless it happens to be objectively perfect. Call this:

NLPsy3.0: Law of antipathy.

The law of antipathy gives rise to *thought* and to *thinking*. Thought and thinking are basically emotions of antipathy. The thing is that under the conditions we have on the surface of this planet, antipathy is a highly creative force. Here, temperatures and pressures are right enough to force what would otherwise drive personalities away from each other into the deep reaches of cosmic space into modalities of transformation and creative adjustment. Hence, multicellular life, human consciousness and social institutions.

Pure conversation is a way to increase the temperature and the pressure on the ego. Everyone knows deep down whether or not they feel perfectly satisfied. In pure conversation, we want to know whether as a matter of fact that condition obtains universally and without exception. We want to base our future social activity on, and only on, a testament to the effect that perfect satisfaction is the actual case.

Under such conditions, the ego will ultimately take up residence outside the body, in the etheric world of cosmic life.

Now suppose someone in the conversation feels he (she) cannot affirm perfect satisfaction with what was just said. What procedure is open to him (her)? It is to *give the social body a directive.* The merest hint of dissatisfaction confers the right (but not the duty) to demand the attention (and the energy) of everyone present. A *request* is always a directive. In pure conversation, however, the request can have only one form – it can only be a request to reproduce the content that just forced its way to the surface or precipitated from the heights. Any other kind of request would violate the numerous principles of social function, including the principles of extensionality, of necessary concatenation and of indifferent expression.

Ultimately, an accurately reproduced content must produce universal satisfaction. There is simply no alternative. As a consequence of an accurate reproduction, either everyone can understand, perhaps better than ever, what was just said and why it was just said, or everyone can understand, perhaps for the first time, the *limitations* under which a speaker is laboring when he (she) says something in the way he (she) does. In this second case, satisfaction may not be with the content of what was just said, but with the context in which it was said, i.e. with the fact that *this particular person said it and was compelled to say it in the way he (she) said it.*

In that way, the membership of the conversational institution *selects itself.* Some people (perhaps all) may decide to continue to work with the people who, despite their limitations, are drawn to their particular social circle. They will feel that charity and the growth of others are the real focus of their own ontological seeking. Others may decide in the future to associate with persons who are able to keep the reference of their speech confined to the *logos* of what everyone has indicated they want to talk about, and nothing else. They will feel that their ontological commitments are more cold-blooded and logical, having to do with existential purposes and the resonances of the starry spaces. In either case, this sorting process is nothing more and nothing less than what goes on all the time anyway in human society. The difference is that with conversation theory, this activity can be made a matter of public record: explicit, self-conscious, subject to general standards of social organization and can begin to be reflected in the public art and culture of that society. Thus,

NLPsy9.0: Law of free association.

Chapter 4

TRUTH

But when he, the Spirit of truth is come, he will teach you all truth.
For he shall not speak of himself. —JOHN 16:13

THIS THEORY OF conversation is a *pragmatic metaphysics*. It is an attempt to engage individuals on the basis of a categorical imperative and make this moral or spiritual necessity the foundation of a specific social form. How a *semantic theory* (a theory of truth conditions) is necessary to implement this program will be suggested here. It may not be superficially clear that the logical meaning of words and sentences is or should be construed as essentially moral or spiritual, but that in essence is the claim. Logical necessity, which is the motivation behind semantic theory, is ultimately the imperative behind conversation theory as well. If this connection between what is meant conversationally and what is morally necessary can be shown convincingly, semantics will become the new spiritual domain, replete with its own set of laws.

It should be noted that conversation theory purports to become the modern vehicle for spiritual initiation. What was once done in the King's Chamber of the Great Pyramid at Cheops, or in the presence of the Grand Priestess at Eluesis or in the intimate company of the Hindu guru and his (her) chela, will in the coming Epoch be accomplished among groups, and even populations, of free individuals adopting the principles of self-conscious conversation. In Western societies, it seems altogether clear, the Age of Faith is to be replaced by the Age of Knowledge, and the exercise of knowledge includes, and in some sense begins with, self-consciousness and self-knowledge. Thus,

CCSIn2.0: Principle of spiritual initiation (real conversation aims at spiritual initiation).

Semantics and Indexicality

There is in contemporary philosophy a great debate as to whether our thoughts are determined ultimately by *sentences expressed*, which have an essentially syntactic character, or by *contextual implication*, which has an essentially intuitive and pragmatic character. Are we, as cognitive intelligences, essentially cold, calculating machines, with the potential for an objective knowledge of the cosmos and of other intelligences in the cosmos? Or are we, as cognitive intelligences, essentially bound to contingent facts about our circumstances, about the cosmos and about our sociological "thrownness" into a world of human products and human expectations?

My answer here, as was Kant's over 200 years ago, is that we are essentially both types of intelligence, and that it is up to us to keep them straight. To the extent we can keep them straight, we can become spiritually free. Spiritual freedom, after all, is represented by a mind which *sees through* all things, both the brute facts of nature and the institutional games of society. Accordingly, this theory lays an equal stress on the *a priori* concepts by which, out of transcendental-logical necessity, all conversation is governed, and on the practical management of those rules in a context that always unfolds uniquely each time it is laid out.

The central semantic notion of conversation theory is that *what is said*, call it p, is determined by a *universal cognitive intuition*. Semantic content is intuition. In pure conversation, everyone recognizes (intuits) p to be true, and only if this is the case can the next proposition, call it q, be attempted. The proposition series (p, q, r... z) thus has an *autonomous character*. No individual speaker or interpreter can determine the reference of the series (p, q, r... z), nor can any individual determine what (p, q, r... z) may actually turn out to be. These determinations are made on a *transcendental basis*. *Everyone's* comportment and intuition contributes to these determinations, and these determinations are constituted by the physical (wave functional) sum of all the moral or spiritual impulses in the room. This transcendental mechanism is a matter of physical and logical necessity.

Although this scenario may appear to be essentially pragmatic, I think there is room for a semantic model theory here. In order to get unambiguous reference out of uninterpreted syntactic streams, modern semantic theory relies on the notion of *indexicality*. On semantic model theory, a term or a predicate is always indexed to a world, a time, a position in space and any number of other possible assignments, in short to a *context*. This system of indexing makes it possible in theory for anyone, even an insensate computer program, to determine the reference and the truth of any uninterpreted syntactic string. These indices or contexts are defined extensionally, as objects and sets, and the outcome of their application to the syntactic item, whether mark, utterance or thought, is likewise an extensional value, a truth or a falsehood. Under such a treatment, the notion of a sentence's or an utterance's meaning, intensionality or implicature more or less evaporates.

For example, the sentence,

(1) Bill is ready

appears to mean, implicate or otherwise intend a set of unexpressed predicates, i.e. those concrete things that Bill is ready for. Without a full disclosure of these predicates in the form of an index of some sort, sentence (1) is both context-dependent and intensional. As such, (1) in theory can have no conversational function because nothing is present to constitute its identical representation in the mind of everyone present. For that condition to be satisfied, either an index or an intension or both will need to be specified – Bill is ready for the exam to be given *this* afternoon in *that* room at *this* time; Bill is ready to wrestle but not ready for Bruno Sammartino. Semantically, the index invoked by "this," "that," and "this," or the intension invoked by "Bruno Sammartino" is a function from a set of circumstances with concrete possibility in the actual world to a truth value. When the appropriate index or intension is assigned, sentence (1) becomes completely transparent or extensional, and everyone's mind will, by a kind of natural or transcendental law, represent it in the same way. Under, and only under this condition can its truth value then be given a social function on the order of a natural law.

In contrast, the sentence,

(2) Billie is pregnant

appears much less to require an index to make it universally intelligible. No woman can be half-pregnant, and sentence (2) makes no claim about Billie in her first, second or third trimesters. Sentence (2) thus has an intrinsic or absolute semantic value. Everyone understands it in the same way, and if Hyp1 is correct, sentence (2) invokes the same mental content in anyone who tries to interpret it. Technically, (2) is *semantically minimal* or *semantically insensitive*. In other words, the meaning of (2) depends on no features of its context of utterance, and on no features of its circumstance of evaluation. Perhaps (2) is even some transcendental object, fixed and unmoving in some higher dimensional space, which everyone intuits (perceives) in the way everyone intuits (perceives) fixed and unmoving objects in this world, Mount Rushmore, for example.

On the present theory, the dissolution of meaning (semantics) into extended context and truth value is rather desirable. The aim of real conversation is not subjective stimulation or deep hidden meaning. The aim of real conversation is cosmic self-knowledge, and the profound states of energy and attention that come with it. Under conditions of pure conversation, no one has time for anything less than a completely unambiguous system of references and a purely extensional presentation and self-presentation. The present theory may serve as the required index or meta-index for such a cooperating society. The list of rules or constitutive expectations outlined here can be applied effectively to any social utterance or self-presentation if and only if everyone concerned is willing and able to do so. As a result of this *a priori* and transcendental index, any utterance or self-presentation in pure conversation will be semantically insensitive, and if not so on the face of it, will be subject to a further explicit index that everyone present uniformly applies and accepts or feels they have accepted. Of course, in the absence of total technological control by means of cameras, sensors and perhaps unrealistically sophisticated computer programming, such uniformity must be left to some very subtle intuitive standards. But regardless of the standards ultimately accepted, the outcome of such a condition can only be the universal experience of social transparency and truth, in short, the experience of a spiritual or cosmic reality. Thus,

> CC$_M$Rat5.0: Principle of the index (principle of logical assignment and logical satisfaction);
> HypSoc3.0: Hypothesis on the conversational index (the theory of conversation).

The metaphysical peculiarity of the particular assignment being put forward in HypSoc3.0 (i.e. in this text itself) is the claim that it is logically *a priori*. The rules and laws enumerated here are supposed to be transcendental, objectively valid and of the type that everyone will want to accept. As such, they are already at work in us and in society. It is just a question of our straightening up enough to apply them systematically and self-consciously to our social circumstances and to ourselves. On the current theory, our self-conscious experience is a purely extensional component in an objective and *a priori* system of cosmic logic, cosmic assignment and cosmic purpose. Thus,

> HypSoc3.1: Hypothesis on cosmic logic (the theory of conversation is cosmic).

Now the key notion in collapsing the moral necessity of well-formed conversation (e.g. indifferent reproducibility, transparent motive, causal reference, universal direction, etc.) into the logical necessity of formal semantics (indexicality, extensionality, predicate constants, truth, etc.) is, once again, *satisfaction*. For conversation theory, satisfaction is a function of *biological intentionality*, the capacity in the organism to *represent* something to itself as a way to adapt to an environment, and as we will see in its highest egoic forms, to entail artistic expression and artistic appreciation. But *semantic satisfaction* is also well-defined. Semantic satisfaction is membership in a set that interprets a formula or syntactic item. Semantic satisfaction is a type of *fit* between possible objects and a system of interpreting heretofore uninterpreted strings. The semantic model is the same sort of thing as the biological model, where only the molecules that fit together spatially are relevant for various cellular functions, although a plethora of otherwise irrelevant molecules may also be present in the soup.

The parallel may be more than analogy. Pure conversation in general is held not for the purpose of rehearsing some pre-determined outcome, but for the purpose of *seeing what materializes*, and both enjoying and profiting from that experience. As conversationists, we are each individually something like molecules bouncing around in a cosmic cytoplasm waiting to achieve a fit or a cognitive synthesis with some other semantically constituted individual or individuals. When that happens, a sort of moral magic happens. Something spiritual, autonomous and profoundly satisfying emerges. That something, of course, is truth itself. Truth is the result of biological intentionalities (cosmic etheric spaces) literally fitting together. The point of conversation theory is to get the cytoplasmic factors right, the pH, the hormonal biases, the membrane potentials. When our intentionalities fit together rightly, the semantic purpose of conversation is realized. Thus:

HypSoc1.0: Idea of reciprocal satisfaction (theory of the semantic cytoplasm).

Now formal semantics can only give us part of the story about the transcendental intuitions at the root of real conversation. Formal semantics, which is a highly technical and mystifying set of logical and terminological definitions, can tell us how to be realistic about Plato's forms. For the rest of the story however, we need to understand biological intentionality *from a first person standpoint*. This first person standpoint is, after all, the position from which the motives of all conversational impulses arise. To understand and appreciate these impulses, we need to understand and appreciate *meaning as we experience it*. In the current text, this understanding is attempted in the chapter on *Intentionality*. For our purposes here, it will suffice to show how the crucial notion of indexicality can be applied to first-person ontologies.

The notion of indexicality can equally be applied to subjective and proprietary domains as it can to objective and language-driven domains, i.e. to society in general. The technique of *jnana yoga*, in which the yogi attempts to transcend the associations of the mind by reminding himself (herself), "Not this, not this," is the paradigm example of the index in action. The spiritual attitude in general is an effort to stay free of the entrapment of illusory impulses, and the index is the primary, and perhaps the only tool available to the human intelligence to do so. The body is full of unnamed and uninterpreted energy gates which open and close in a manner inaccessible to an undeveloped self-consciousness. It is incumbent on every conversational aspirant to develop a bodily index, a familiarity with the limitations and capabilities of his (her) own energy system, and to apply this index to every moment of both proprietary and social self-consciousness. Thus,

CC$_\text{M}$Rat5.1: Principle of the self-conscious index (principle of *jnana yoga*).

The Concept of Truth

The concept of truth, when used in religious, magical and mystical contexts, is rather vague. There, by and large, it appears to mean "reality" or something like "God." Christ, the magician of the ages, for example, says,

And ye shall know the truth, and the truth shall set you free. (John 8:32)

Presumably the term "truth" here refers to some general condition of existence rather than a correspondence of some sort between sentences or assertions and facts about the world. Similarly, the Buddha recommends the following procedure:

Filled with faith he visits him and pays respect to him; having paid respect to him, he gives ear; when he gives ear, he hears the Dharma; having heard the Dharma, he memorizes it and examines the meaning of the teachings he has memorized;

when he examines their meaning, he gains a reflective acceptance of those teachings; when he gains a reflective acceptance
of those teachings, zeal springs up; when zeal has sprung up,
he applies his will; having applied his will, he scrutinizes; having scrutinized, he strives; resolutely striving, he realizes with
the body the ultimate truth and sees it by penetrating it with
wisdom. (Pali Canon)

Aurobindo, the Hindu-Indian philosopher of spiritual and social evolution, is a little more precise about what sorts of things can
be true, but the tendency is still to view truth as an absolute, and
not as a relationship between statements and spatial realities, outer
or inner:

Mankind seems now indeed inclined to grow a little modester
and wiser; we no longer slay our fellows in the name of God's
truth or because they have minds differently trained or differently constituted from ours; we are less ready to curse and
revile our neighbour because he is wicked or presumptuous
enough to differ from us in opinion; we are ready even to admit that Truth is everywhere and cannot be our sole monopo-
ly; we are beginning to look at other religions and philosophies
for the truth and help they contain and no longer merely in
order to damn them as false or criticize what we conceive to be
their errors. (*Essays on the Gita*)

As for Plato's Socrates, whose life and whose death for the sake
of socially realized truth is exceeded in world literature only by that
of Christ himself, truth is the standard to which all discourse and all
conversation must aspire and ultimately must conform:

If we are to adopt this method (of conversation), it must be
on the condition that we all regard ourselves as rivals in the
attempt to distinguish truth from falsehood. We are each
equally concerned in the truth being made clear. I will tell you
my conclusions, but if any of you think I am allowing myself
to assume what is not true, he must interrupt and challenge
me. I am not speaking dogmatically from the certainty of
assured knowledge. I will never claim that. I am simply

your fellow explorer in the search for truth. If somebody contradicts me and is obviously right, I will be the first to give way. (*Gorgias*)

Truth pursued is the Socratic doctrine of conversation, and all are at once humbled and uplifted by its discovery. A life which neglects this progressive method of intercourse is devoid of value, and a life which adheres faithfully to its rigors finds itself wanting no other outcome, and no alternative:

> For I tell you, that to let no day pass without discussing goodness and all the other subjects about which you hear me talking and examining both myself and others, this is really the very best thing that a man can do, and that life without this sort of examination is not worth living. (*Apology*)

In Plato, truth is an ultimate good for the human being, perfecting and leading his (her) soul into a supersensible existence beyond this one, and bringing him (her) closer to God and to the cosmic hierarchies whose concerted actions stand at his (her) very origin.

The modern concept of truth is, by contrast, a direct outgrowth of the concept of logic. Intelligence as we know it and understand it is based in principle on this sort of usage. Logical statements are either true or false; logical circuits in computers and other intelligent servers receive bivalent inputs (either "yes" or "no") and return an equivalent type of output; the neurons of the brain and nervous system likewise function on the basis of an all-or-none principle, at least insofar as their action potentials are concerned. A bivalent value system in large part also defines conversation, which is a form of social intelligence. Conversation, in its modern conception, and for better or for worse, is a concatenation of *judgments* (truth functional predicates) which, under ideal conditions, *all return the value T (true)*.

Judgments are locutions with the form:

(1) A is B.

and as such return the values True or False. These locutions appear to be the only real candidates for conversation. Given the nature of our sensorium, and the level of our material culture, judgments are the only way we have to open ourselves to the reality of our day to day existence, They are the means by which we find it possible, as rational beings, to function in the world with a certain degree of competence, and thereby to create it. The judgments we make by and large constitute our reality.

It appears necessary that only true judgments can constitute pure conversation. Neither a series of false judgments, nor a series of judgments with at least one false token could survive the test of universal satisfaction. From a pragmatic standpoint, therefore, any judgment that does survive that test might as well be called true. As far as conversation theory is concerned, universal satisfaction among participants is truth. Let us say:

> CCTr1.0: Only true judgments are allowed in conversation (principle of truth);
> CCTr2.0: Truth is universal satisfaction (principle of pragmatism).

The Geometry of Reality

The important thing about truth, of course, is that, however it is understood, it has something important to do with *reality*. Modern logicians by and large consider statements to be true which correspond somehow to reality. Conversation is always and only (or should be always and only) a disclosure of reality itself to those who conjure the conversation.

If we follow Kant, we should say that "reality" basically means existence in time, or in general, sensation. This is Kant's analysis, in the *Schematism*, of what the *a priori* rational conception of reality is. But if we relax our standards a little, not insisting on too tight a logical or physical argument, we should probably not be far off to consider reality to be a property of *space*. True statements therefore correspond to, or perhaps sometimes even coincide with, relationships in space.

Now relationships in space are described by *geometry*. Most practical geometry today is based on the *measurement* of lengths and angles, and from this practice arises modern engineering in all of its amazing, but ultimately unsatisfying guises. We live in a world whose outer form and many of whose values are dominated by applications of this kind of geometry. But there is a branch of geometry, some would say it is the actual root of geometry, wherein no measurements are made, but only precise drawings are made and the relationships arising within those drawings are studied. This is called *synthetic* or *projective geometry*. It is this kind of geometry, this kind of space and this kind of reality that the practice of conversational truth is about.

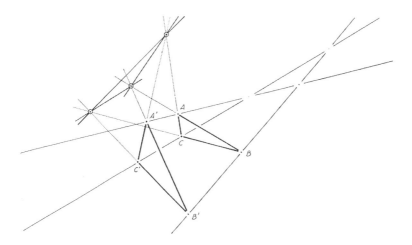

Figure 4: Two triangles not in Desargue's relationship

Draw two triangles and relate them by pairing their points and their sides (the points AA', BB', CC'; the sides aa', bb', cc'). Now look for the three points in which the pairs of sides meet and the three lines common to the point-pairs. It will usually happen that the lines joining AA', BB' and CC' will somewhere form another triangle of lines (in projective geometry, we take the whole extent of lines into account) while the three points determined by the paired lines (AB, A'B'; AC, A'C'; BC, B'C') will also form a triangle (of points) (Figure 4).

The French architect and geometer Girard Desargues (1593–1662) showed that if the triangles are so arranged that the three lines given by the points of the two triangles lie in a point, the pairs of lines of the two triangles will lie in a line, and vice versa (Figure 5). Moreover, this relationship will hold for any two triangles, whether they lie at random in a plane or anywhere in the whole of space (Figure 6)! In producing these triangles, the only rule to be observed is accuracy in rendering; apart from this, there is complete freedom. These triangles can even be constructed using the etheric body, on the channels of the *ida*, *pingala* and *sushumna*, so long as the meditator's consciousness is sufficiently stable, and the geometrical law can be sensed as an energetic reality. In conversation, analogous constructions are possible.

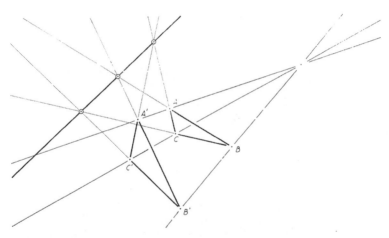

Figure 5: Two triangles in Desargues' relationship

Blaise Pascal (1623–1662), Desargues' famous pupil, contributed substantially to the theory of conic sections (circles, ellipses, parabolas, hyperbolas), and discovered a general law of the hexagon at the age of sixteen. Take any six points in a plane and join them in any successive order, but return to the point from which you started. This may generate a familiar-looking hexagon (Figure 7) or something a bit unusual (Figure 8), but either one will be called a "hexagon." Now pair the lines "oppositely": the first with the fourth, the second with

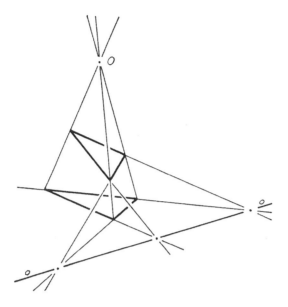

Figure 6: Two triangles not in a plane but in Desargues' relationship

the fifth, the third with the sixth. Extend the line pairs and notice where they fall. If they fall on a line, the hexagon falls on a conic; if they fall on a triangle, the hexagon does not fall on a conic. *If and only if a hexagon is drawn through any six points of a conic, the three meeting points of the "opposite" line pairs will be on a line.*

The remarkable thing about Pascal's theorem is that given any conic (circle, ellipse, parabola or hyperbola), we can choose the six points freely, *anywhere* on the curve, and can join them in *any* cyclic order. The points in which the "opposite" pairs of lines meet will always be in a line! This is called the *polar line* or the *Pascal line,* and all conic hexagrams have one. Some mystical law lies behind this freedom, and Pascal called his conic figure the *Hexagrammum Mysticum.*

Now in both Desarges' and Pascal's theorems we have lawful properties of space arising not from measurements but from *relationships in space*, and from the protocol that gave order to those relationships. Pure conversation will eventually be understood, I think, to work in exactly the same way. In conversation, however, the spaces

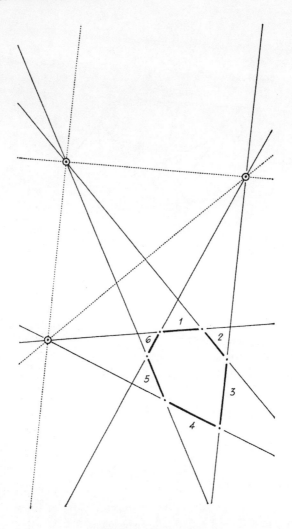

Figure 7: A hexagon not in a conic section

are considerably more complicated than those of these examples. In conversation, the important spaces are *inside the human body*, inside the cavities and hollows of the living mass. It is the purpose of conversational protocol to adjust the alignments and vector spaces of this living mass and to give it a subtle order so that the relationships within these spaces can work their projective magic. The laws

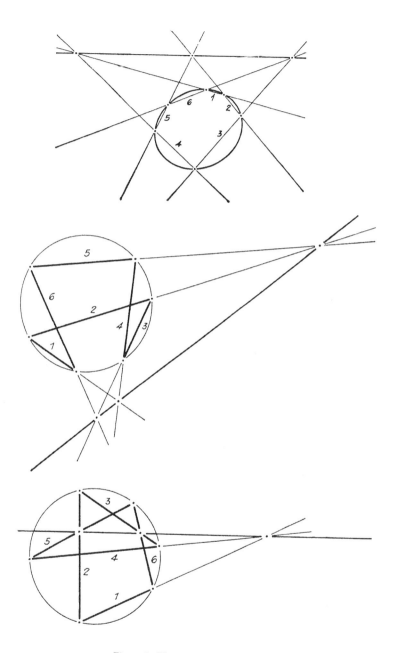

Figure 8: Hexagons in a conic section

of these projective or synthetic relationships are then disclosed to the conversational witnesses (also the participants) by *energy effects* and *imaginative cognition*.

Now it is not altogether accurate to say that the important spaces in conversation are inside people's joints and bodily cavities. These are just the ones that are most in need of being pointed out and exercised. The external spaces are also very important. These are the spaces in which our etheric bodies can make contact with each other, and lead to supersensible impressions of the reality of our consciousness. These spaces are also ordered by conversational protocol, and can be made subject to law and lawful relationships on their own account. For example, Aristotle's ratio, 1.618… can be built in to these external spaces by requiring the conversational exchange to trace a pentagram (which, if well-formed, contains this ratio in an infinity of iterations) over the surface of the earth.

Now the question arises quite naturally as to how it is possible for these mystical moments and supersensible impressions to be generated out of spatial alignments projected to great, middle range or miniscule distances. Do these moments arise in a chemical or cookbook fashion, in which the procedure, if executed properly, is sufficient for material results, and if miscued, undermined or otherwise botched leads to no interesting result? If this is the case, how far does the geometrical analog go? What, for example in a living conversation, is the drafting board, what is the straight edge and what is the pencil? What binds the spaces of conversation together and makes applying the reality procedures (the truth procedures) of pure conversation feasible in the first place?

The basic answer to this last question is that conversation depends on individuals with a clear and unsullied *sense of self*. It may prove to be that all of the rules purporting to constitute pure conversation, of which I believe there may be tens of thousands, are really rules making it possible to decide by literal tests who in conversation has this self sense and who does not. A clear and unsullied sense of self is perfectly apparent to him (her) who has crossed the threshold of spiritual enlightenment, but is subject to all manner of presumption, misrepresentation and fantasy by him (her) who has not. But who is to say who has the correct perception of whose sense of self is in fact unsullied? Conversational rules and conversation theory in general are intended to make consensual judgments about these heretofore intractable matters possible.

As for the first set of questions, I leave the answers to future research. To answer them we will need a quantified study of human energy, including esoteric conceptions of the subtle bodies, as well as a precise usage of concepts of intentionality, the theory of action and rationality in action. Suffice it to say that there are probably more than three spatial dimensions involved in human consciousness, and that the geometrical analog of supersensible intuition involves the projection of figures in higher dimensions into a consciousness adapted to lower ones.

It is the sense of self then, universally quantified, that makes a study of the projective relationships in the spaces of conversation, and their energetic and cognitive effects, possible. Assume a group of people are gathered for conversation, and assume they are each spiritually adept (i.e. assume they have each somehow passed the threshold of death, each have a real sense of self, and each know the difference in general between reality and illusion). Assume their motivation in coming together is to enjoy the wonder of truth, and the reality of existence, and to exercise their individual freedom.

Under these conditions, the conversation actually begins many hours or days before the actual convocation, when the time of the conversation and its theme are named, and the preparation phase is initiated. At once in the formality of gathering, all of the spatial relationships, inner and outer, from the order of people's appearance, to the disposition of the seating, to the gestures and acknowledgments of one another, tacit or explicit, to the first words spoken and their resonance characteristics, to the impulses to speak and to think, to the mood and atmosphere of the meeting are determined and made ready for study. The purpose of the conversational protocol is to hold that prepared space, which is extremely complex, constant and to keep it from being degraded by carelessness. The projective relationships that are intrinsic to the situation are a property of the truth value of each iteration of the conversational algorithm. They are inscribed in the etheric and astral bodies of the selves who have come together to exercise their freedom, and are read out of the ether by supersensible intuition.

Now projective geometry makes particular use of a geometrical location that cannot be drawn, or even sensed, but that can only be conceived. This is the location infinitely distant from us, where points, lines, planes and even solids can reside and make their influence felt in our local corner of the cosmos. Geometrical constructions can include this location, and even though doing this often makes familiar objects, such as a triangle with one vertex at infinity, appear unfamiliar, the laws that hold for our familiar triangles hold likewise for these unfamiliar figures. Desargues' two triangle theorem, for example, holds equally for two triangles, one of which has one of its vertices placed at infinity (Figure 9).

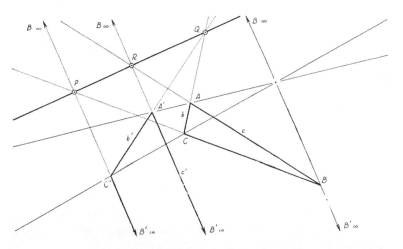

Figure 9: Desargues' relationship, but with one triangle with one vertex at infinity

It is axiomatic in geometry that parallel lines meet at a unique point at infinity. Likewise, parallel planes meet at an infinitely distant line that is perfectly straight. There is a plane at infinity with its own remarkable properties, and there are probably solid objects that can be conceived to lie at infinity. The inner spaces of the human body, when lined up properly, can come into geometrical (projective) relationship with these infinitely distant objects, and can undergo lawlike changes in response to that relationship. Those changes can be sensed in energetic effects and in supersensible cognitions. Language, properly used, is sufficient to effect those alignments. That, at least, is the theory. Let us say:

> HypPsy2.0: Hypothesis on projective geometry (theory of the ideal forms);
> HypPsy2.1: Principle of the self.

Now we have a way to begin to make sense of this rather baffling conception of truth. Truth is correspondence to or coincidence with relationships in space, and this space can include both the infinitely distant and the infinitesimally small. At the same time, truth is constituted by universal acceptance. It is a bivalent social value. A proposition is true if and only if everyone thinks (or can think) that it is true. Truth, like the pictorial laws of modern geometry, is based on relationships in space rather than on measurable quantities. Truth, like the mystery of psychedelic experience, is a capacity in the human being for objective linkage to the cosmos itself.

Now we can turn to Christ's description of what this condition signifies:

> But when he, the Spirit of truth, is come, he will teach you all truth. For he shall not speak of himself; but what things soever he shall hear, he shall speak; and the things that are to come, he shall shew you. (John 16:13)

On the one hand, the Spirit of truth simply reproduces what he hears; on the other, he gives clairvoyant vision to everyone concerned. The Spirit of truth is the *logos*, the logic of conversation under the rules of universal satisfaction. It ("he") is the unique and ineffable content that satisfies the human being perfectly. It ("he") is the tremendous cosmic impulse to build a literal City of spirits in the material world of atoms, stars and circling planets. It ("he") is the unified and awakened will in the human being, which still lies sleeping in the Body of man, but which, as a law of nature, has moved all human history on an unmistakable trajectory of cultural, political and scientific progress and betterment. Call this:

CCTr2.1: Principle of *logos* (principle of the spirit of truth).

Chapter 5

Freedom

Nothing is freer than the imagination. —HUME

The imagination is built up out of something universal that functions as a rule. —KANT

THE MOST PREDICTABLE objection to a theory of conversation comes from the assertion of freedom. How can a long and exhaustive list of rules (conditions on expression) be anything but an attempt to limit freedom, to reduce it to mechanicality and the realm of mere nature? What could be more nefarious and diabolical than to attempt to judge and control the impulses of thought and imagination, manifestly the freest things in God's creation, on the basis of man-made rules, or even on the basis of cosmic laws, if that argument could be made plausible?

The reply is to establish the real nature of human freedom and to proceed on that basis. Following Kant, we say that freedom in general is *law accepted willingly*. This formula may seem paradoxical, but if one thinks about it enough, one concludes that it is the correct picture. Human freedom is always a matter of representing a rule (a concept) to oneself, deciding if one likes it, and if one does, using the rule (the concept) as if it were one's own in order to will a certain action. Human freedom is intuitive judgment.

On this picture, it doesn't matter where the rule one applies ultimately comes from, or if the person himself (herself) was responsible for thinking it up. Nor does it matter what further rules a person may apply in deciding to appropriate it. All that matters is whether or not the person is sympathetic with it in the moment he (she) uses it. Does he (she) like the judgment the rule suggests, or not? If yes, the action is free; if no, the action is not free.

The Random Consideration Generator

Notwithstanding these transcendental, Wittgensteinian considerations, it is important to begin an explanation of freedom on a mechanical level, because it is at this level that our intuitions are most likely to agree. The contemporary philosopher Daniel Dennett (b. 1942) has given us something substantial to explain a certain aspect of the free will, an engineering model that fits nicely with everything we know and understand about the mind, about causation and about intentional actions. Dennett's model introduces modal notions into John Searle's naturalistic picture of the free will, where a gap between a decision to act and a bodily movement constitutes our actual freedom. When extended, it also specifies the crucial factor of having reasons for a free action, and accounts for the counterfactual sense that other actions could have been taken in place of the one that actually was.

I will not rehearse here the range of virtues of Dennett's idea—that it allows selective intelligence to make a difference in free actions, that it gives moral education a sense and a significance, that it appears able to account for the fact that thought impulses are somewhat discontinuous and unpredictable, etc.—but will focus on one shortcoming a recent Berkeley seminar seemed to identify. Dennett describes no mechanism to override the output of a *random consideration generator* embedded in the brain. Once a preference has been selected from the generator's output at time t_1, what prevents another series of considerations from pushing into consciousness at time t_2? Why aren't free decisions a kind of random walk as one decision, then another and then yet another each temporarily hold sway?

The answer here of course is that sometimes it actually is like that. But usually it is not, and in these cases something in us doesn't want to give attention to the generator's output once a decision is made. A certain will takes over. Dennett actually recognizes this, pointing out that the generator is typically active in moments of lazy mulling, rather than in periods of intensive concentration. Put the other way around, something in us becomes sympathetic with one of the representations the generator produces. If we make a decision, at some level we like that decision. We judge it to be ok, *the best of all possibilities*. In short, we universalize it. This sympathetic will is what Searle analyzes as the *causal self-reference* of the intention in action. The intention in action has conditions of satisfaction *that this very intention, and no other, causes*, say, consideration c_4 to represent my decision. Causal self-reference is the sympathetic will, and it is sufficient to override the output of the generator. Let us say:

> HypPsy4.0: Hypothesis on the random generator;
> HypPsy5.0: Hypothesis on causal self-reference (the theory of
>   the sympathetic will)

No wonder we have the feeling of a free will! The free will is doubly determined. At one stage in the neurological cascade, its content devolves from a random generator, and is thereby subject to no causal pattern. It appears to come from out of nowhere. At another, more important stage, this content is something with which we become necessarily sympathetic, and thereby is something we automatically accept *because it is ours*. Both this condition of a content's being sympathetic to us and our automatic acceptance of it is intrinsic to its formal universality. Also intrinsic to this universality are our momentary sense of selfhood and our sense of freedom. This universal content is something that to us in the moment seems objectively valid, correct or otherwise right, *all things considered*. It is the value or moral imperative we see in the action. It is our reason for doing what we do.

Freedom as Imaginative Judgment

Consider a social situation, negative or even apparently positive, in which the agent is at a loss for words. He (she) literally does not know what to say next, and only has recourse to a platitude, to a change of subject or to an awkward or painful silence. These are moments in which there is no personal freedom. In such moments, life becomes stagnant, even toxic, and of negative value. The soul, whether or not it knows it, will require purification of its accumulated by-products. On the other hand, if a person has recourse to some concept (rule) which he (she) can unambiguously apply to the situation, and applies it acceptably to everyone, then he (she) remains free and undegraded, regardless how distasteful or hypocritical the company is.

Suppose for example I am a military operative captured behind enemy lines, and am brought to an interrogating room. My captors know I have some important information, and they proceed to elicit this from me by asking me questions. But suppose these captors are particularly ethical, and adhere to some enlightened conventions of warfare, absolutely abjuring torture and other methods of coercion. Suppose I know as a matter of fact that in the last resort, they will accept the name, rank and serial number of any captured enemy, regardless of how important or vital this enemy's information may be.

If under these conditions I am required to speak, and I simply repeat my name, rank and serial number, I remain free in an important sense. My body may not be free (I am captured) but my mind will be free. If in my situation I can apply the concept of conventional identification, and apply it in a way that everyone has to accept, I will remain substantially free because *I will have nothing to worry about.*

But if my captors suspend their use of the rules of capture, and start trying to coerce me with threats and with tortures I am unprepared for, then my freedom will be substantially compromised. Now motivated by fear and dread, my mind will be under continual and heavy stress. If I reach the *limits of what I am able to imagine* (the limits of my judgment), and am simultaneously denied a way to transcend the terror of my captors' malice, my mind will break down to a sub-human state of animality or vegetation. Soon thereafter, I am likely to divulge my secrets to them. That at any rate is the basic theory of brainwashing, torture and political and military coercion. These techniques are predicated on the absolute removal of freedom. Thus,

CCJ1.1.2: Principle of judgment (judgment as freedom).

Freedom as Sympathetic Will

The basic psychological idea here is that the human mind, including its higher spiritual modalities of imagination and cosmic intuition, is free to the extent it finds it possible to *recognize* what it contains. To recognize something is to apply a rule or a concept to it. It is, in a sense, to measure the object, to size it up, to describe it and thus to bring it, in that aspect, under the sovereignty or power of the free agent (the ego) who bears witness to it. All mental contents have this feature of *fitting in* with a pattern, rule or concept that is already there in the mind and that the mind in an important way actually gives them. Any content in the mind which cannot fit in with or be recognized by some prior template of rules, concepts or schemata is an impossibility.

In general, education works along just these lines. Place the erstwhile captive in a classroom and give him (her) material which challenges his (her) imagination to the point where he (she) must exercise his (her) willpower to stay on top of the situation, and you have the basic model of human learning and intellectual growth. Education is predicated on the human need for freedom, and the rationalization of modern society, which devolves in large part from its educational system, is a consequence of the social classifications that emerge from individuals applying their spiritual capacities to the idea of freedom.

The same procedure was the basis of the kingly and priestly initiations of ancient civilizations, but here a total removal of freedom was spiritually ampliative. Here the initiate, after months and years of preparation, was placed, for example, in the King's Chamber of the Great Pyramid at Cheops. Alone in the darkness, his mind and inner vision were, at some point, brought into total and all-embracing contact with a reality wholly unknown to him (her). In this moment, no judgment was possible for him (her), and a great gesture of freedom (a great spiritual gesture) was required for him (her) to survive the experience. Passing through the *gate of fear* in this controlled manner permanently altered the alignment of the initiate's subtle bodies, and gave him (her) direct knowledge of the cosmos itself.

The purpose of kingly initiation, of course, was not the mere coercion and exploitation of someone's mind, nor was it intellectual development. It was rather to make the mind of one man, the king or pharaoh, cosmically powerful and free above all others. By means of the constructive techniques of kingly initiation, the lesser freedom intrinsic to a rational and healthy human being was supplanted or rather was augmented by the greater freedom of cosmic knowledge, ontological certainty and coincidence (sympathy) with the forces and laws of nature herself. With the presence of an initiate bearing the consciousness and the divine rights of kingship, society could be effectively organized.

In either case, whether one's freedom is great and turned to matters of cosmic importance, or whether it is common and turned to ordinary matters of decision and discrimination, freedom is a matter of will. The initiation of the priest or king was something he (she) undertook and sustained willingly. Under no other conditions could the initiation proceed. The cosmological actions of a divinely annointed agent were likewise willed by himself (herself). Similarly, whenever a modern intellectual and democratically informed consciousness, free and sovereign over his (her) own decisions in, for example, matters of career choice, takes a particular social action, he (she) does so *because he (she) wants to.* He (she) fits himself (herself) to his (her) action by accepting in sympathy the rule (the concept) that that action suggests or must suggest to his (her) rational mind. Let us therefore say:

NLPsy5.0: Law of sympathy (law of the free will).

Freedom as Well-Ordered Expectation

In general on a chess board, a checkmated king is not free because there are no squares available to it into which to move. But in chess, an *absolute removal of freedom* is rare. A chess player is almost always free to resign a position. An analogous situation obtains in conversation, but with some important qualifications. On the one hand, even the side with severely diminished prospects on the chessboard remains free to the extent some sort of move, however hopeless, is possible for him (her). Even the most dim-witted conversationist is in this position. On the other hand, in conversation, checkmate of some hapless individual is not the objective. Rather, freedom itself is the objective. Conversation is exaltation in a universally distributed and reciprocally produced freedom.

Nevertheless, the analogy between conversation and chess has some instructive features. Freedom on the chessboard comes into existence because chess has *well-formed rules.* These rules not only make the game possible in itself, but they order the pragmatic expectations which it is possible to have about any particular situation and about one's position in it. These expectations in themselves represent a kind of *second-order rule.* No one who plays chess seriously, unless he has a surprise planned, will move his queen to a square where it can be captured on the next move. A disinterested observer can make good predictions about the moves on the board based on knowledge of both these first- and second-order rules or expectations. The ability to make these good moves amounts to a type of freedom or power that the chess player enjoys.

I think it is more or less clear that in chess, the side which manipulates the rules and expectations in a way to win the game is granted the maximal freedom. In conversation, in contrast, *everyone is supposed to win.* The conversational model I am proposing has a function analogous to the rules of chess, except that the game is different in kind. By means of this model, not only can one begin to have expectations about and an understanding of the first-order features of the conversational game, its temporal and spatial circumscriptions, for example, but one can also begin to judge the soundness of a particular conversational utterance, whether and how it gives rise to *legitimate conversational expectations,* and in this way to qualify and index individuals for participation in the game. Thus,

CCJ1.1.1: Principle of expectation (the social nature of rules).

Freedom as Absorption

Now all conversational actions are free. They are willed by means of a sympathy for the rule, concept or expectational set they express to the mind of the actor. At no point in conversation, before, during or after, is it suggested or determined with what contents in the substantial conversation one's sympathies should lie. This means:

> CCFr1.0: In conversation, everyone is always free to say whatever he (she) wants to say (principle of freedom).

Pure conversation is orderly and lawful despite the anarchy implied by CCFr1.0, because there are conditions on what someone *can want to say*! The remarkable and paradoxical fact is that there is a *law of freedom*. In conversation, and in human society in general, freedom always takes a definite form and in general terms, that form is *unity*. Now with reference solely to individual motives, the important unity is the unity of consciousness, the transcendental unity of having a rational (descriptive, linguistic) attitude toward ideas and things in the world. Rational beings (personalities) are intrinsically free beings. With reference to conversation, the relevant unity is social. It is the unity of absorption in the living force intrinsic to a functioning and healthy *social organism*. Thus,

> NLSem3.011: Law of the social organism (law of absorption).

Why should absorption in a matrix of energy and higher order function constitute freedom? Does it make sense to think of a liver or a kidney in a healthy body as free in some sense? The answer of course is no insofar as these organs are incapable of rational thought, but in a sense it is yes if they are not diseased and participate in (and contribute to) an overall condition of well-being. The kidney, under these conditions, is free to filter the blood; the liver is free to manufacture glycogen. Freedom from disease and impediments to one's natural function is a kind of freedom.

The situation with the higher spiritual personalities in the cosmos, if disbelief in the possibility or a blind faith in the actuality of their existence is suspended, is probably analogous. The Seraphim, whose sole purpose and end is to glorify God, owing no doubt to their proximity to the ineffable One, are free in the sense that their existence is a matter of pure enjoyment and unimpeded functionality.

But if these personalities, if that is really what they are, never exercise any judgment or reason in the performance of their duties, then they are not free in any interesting sense. It is not my place here to assert what state of affairs actually obtains in this exalted Domain of Ends, because I see no way to decide what these conditions are without some experimentation and justified consensuality. But I do think the model is a good one for pure conversation, where regulated freedom is the essence of the project.

Now livers and kidneys aside, there is good reason to think that a *brain*, indifferently absorbed in the healthful and blissful pulsations of blood, spinal fluid, and the liberal secretion of endorphins, is meaningfully free. This is because the brain and central nervous system are *responsible* in large degree for just this condition of bliss. Responsible control is the necessary condition on freedom, and responsible control is always rational. If brains can be held responsible for conditions inside and outside the body, then brains, which are clearly members of a larger organism, can be free merely in virtue of performing their function well. Thus,

CCSR1.0: Principle of responsible control (principle of responsibility).

A similar analysis holds for conversation, but here the responsible agent is the ego (the self), which at a minimum in its self-conscious form is a *spiritual* entity. The function of the ego is to love. If the ego in conversation loves well, that person, and all others in significant degree, are made free in this social sense of blissful absorption. Responsible control in conversation is given by the social contract, i.e. by rational egos, and by the maxims for action that those egos creatively apply, in the manner of a template, to the conversational moment. The conversational template (e.g. the conversational algorithm, CCLog2.1) is the logical essence of love itself.

Now absorption in a matrix of love, energy and blissfulness bears a certain resemblance to the conditions of drug addiction. I fully anticipate the phenomenon of *passive conversationists*, individuals who participate in conversation merely in order to enjoy the energy pulsing from the more active and responsible segments of the social organism. The situation is analogous to the bhakti yoga taught by Indian saints, and I see nothing wrong with it, as long as the external politics (the power relationships and the general order of society) are correct. A personality enjoying the intoxication of a drug for the moment is free. The problem with exogenous drugs, of course, is that serious imbalances to the system follow, and those imbalances are very compromising to future freedom and moral action. But with endogenous intoxication, which is a feature of well-formed conversation, no such imbalances occur. Even the fully passive participant is carried along in a healthy, if somewhat morally degenerate way.

Freedom as Spatial Competence

I believe that future research based in conversation theory will show that the *a priori* mental templates (concepts) required for free actions are nothing more and nothing less than *spatial relationships* within and outside the human body. They are small and middle range lacunae inside the body and middle range and large spaces outside the body that are coded and calculated, in the manner of a universal Turing machine, by the peripheral and central nervous systems of the human body. The creative intuition, the impulse for original speech and for original understanding, and the experience of the dream are each a literal summation and calculation of physical spaces intended by the human form and extending beyond that form by means of the organs of sense. If the nervous system substantially recognizes those spaces, most of which share the same basic form from individual to individual, the new content is conceptualized and codified according to a universal rule, and that rule in essence is descriptive or linguistic.

Spatial competence of the most natural and commonplace kind was described by Rousseau as the basic sense of freedom. In benign nature, because he simply moves from one location to the next in the way his inclinations and preferences lead him, man is free. He is *free from* restriction. This is the sense of freedom developed by Locke and the English liberals in their theories of government, and certainly it is fundamental to the idea of freedom. But in conversation and in subjective experience generally, the sense of freedom or its lack is all-pervading, encompassing not only the extensionality of nature, architecture and bodies in relationship, but also the intensionality of other people's thoughts. In degenerate society, these negative spaces are highly cultic and inhibiting, but in truly social circumstances they are purifying, ennobling and ecstatic.

P. D. Ouspensky, in his brilliant *Tertium Organum* (1911), is at pains to show that the capacity for concepts (rules), which is an ability occurring only in human beings, and in no form of animal life, is the capacity to grasp the *third dimension of space*. Human experience transcends animal experience in precisely the respect that it can grasp spatial relationships in three dimensions, whereas the animal can only project them onto two dimensions. Conversation theory, which is basically an extension of meditation techniques into linguistic usage, proposes to hold this capacity for experiencing space in three dimensions constant, and to make it possible to examine its actual structure and function. Doing so will allow the spatial relationships that are otherwise unnoticed or consigned to individual occult experience to make themselves known, thus projecting human experience into a super-human and purely social modality, and exhibiting the true extent and structure of human freedom. Thus,

HypPhy2.1: Hypothesis on physical space.

Freedom as the Fourth Dimension

The great conundrum of classical geometry is, "In what direction does the fourth dimension lie?" By extension, we might wonder, "If our consciousness were four dimensional, what would it be like?" I think answers to these questions can be developed through conversation theory. Moreover, I think the answers here in basic outline are fairly straightforward.

Let us take it as axiomatic that we do not in general have much control over our energy. Here I am thinking, of course, of the energy of attention, the energy that jumps around in our mind from focus to focus and that is rarely sustained except under conditions of great exigency. When such exigency is not present, as it usually is not, our minds run along like out-of-control machines. Given this ontological situation, which one could hardly call free, I think it is fairly evident where the fourth dimension is. The fourth dimension lies in the direction of contiguous and self-conscious attention. It lies, in other words, in the direction of real self-consciousness. The fourth dimension is the potential in the human being to be lawfully and healthfully self-conscious, and incidentally, to be spiritually free.

Where is the fourth dimension? We go there every time we sleep deeply. To be sure, we have no memory of it because our consciousness is not adapted to it (it is, after all, perpendicular to everything we know in the sense world) but actually we know it very well. It is our intrinsic freedom. Just as in one dimension (in a line) a point has one degree of freedom, in two dimensions (in a plane) a point has two degrees of freedom, and in three dimensions (in physical space) a point has three degrees of freedom, so in four dimensions (in space-time) a cosmic individual has four degrees of freedom. Cosmic (spiritual) freedom is dimensionality, and its freedom is incommensurably greater than any freedom we may achieve in the three dimensional world of the senses.

What is it like there? In a word, it is ecstatic. It is unbelievably intense and realistic, with all manner of fantastic lines and characters, some wonderful and some horrible, manifesting with each moment of self-consciousness. There is no sense of time, and no real sense of space, for that matter, but only imagination and vision. But more than that, there is the sense of *material reality*. There is the sense that material reality is being brought into being simply in virtue of one's having a sense of self, and a deep and contiguous stream of energy and attention. There is the sense of a pre-existing cosmic condition in which all ontological relationships are transparent and all ontological judgments are unnecessary.

If the fourth dimension, the realm sought by the drug addict, by the schizophrenic and by the meditator alike, is the realm of deep sleep brought to self-conscious awareness, then pure conversation is the vehicle by which to enter that realm by social law, scientific protocol and sensible and systematic exploration. The world of three dimensions is given by language, by the rules and expectations that attend the social use of concepts. The world of four dimensions can be given by holding those rules and expectations completely constant, by making society itself the object of inquiry, and seeing what lies behind all of that. This intervention can not be accomplished until the attention of the mind is given a place where it can rest expectantly from moment to moment, until the higher world (or the world in its higher dimension) materializes from out of nowhere.

It is instructive to see how higher dimensional spaces are built up out of lower ones. To build a one dimensional space, which is a line, one takes a zero dimensional space, which is a point, and moves it uniformly in a single direction that is not contained inside it. The result is the series of points that make up a line. Similarly with the construction of a plane from a series of lines moved perpendicular to its own direction, and the construction of a three dimensional space from a series of planes moved in the direction of the remaining perpendicular. Something similar can occur in the human body during meditative concentration and energy practices such as Chinese chi kung. The proprioceptive sense can be used to cast a figure using points in the body (usually along the spine) connected energetically through the body's breath and sustained over time. The result can be an intuitive opening into what can only be presumed to be the fourth dimension.

In conversation this energetic connection and tracing is achieved and sustained not so much through the force of will as through the connectivity intrinsic to well-ordered language use. The "penumbra" of meaning can be used to accomplish a similar movement of the three dimensional figure (the inner sense of the body) into and along a dimension that waking consciousness is not in general adapted to. To be sure, a certain degree of relaxation and mutual good will is required, as well as a certain openness of mental attitude and a uniform application of the formal requirements of real conversation. Under these conditions, not just the individual, but everyone present in the conversation can experience an opening, presumably to the same fourth dimension, and to its attendant freedom. Let us say:

HypPhy5.0: Theory of the fourth dimension.

Freedom as Love of Action

Now if we assemble all of the foregoing guises under which freedom may appear, we produce a picture of future earth evolution as grand in conception as any ever imagined. On Rudolf Steiner's clairvoyant vision, the human presence on earth in the future will be marked by a physical residue left in space and in color of all the movements made by the free and self-conscious activity of the human body. In the future, our individual (i.e. free) intentions, motives and bodily movements in space will build a cosmic hologram in coherent light on top of the material nature of Earth that will lead to our eventual absorption in the supersensible order of reality that we now know only before birth, after death and during dreamless sleep. Our society will extrude this hologram.

Pure conversation requires free moral action of everyone participating. Free moral action in conversation is the love of the conversational deed. In pure conversation, it is not only possible, but it is required, that a condition of love obtain. This condition of universal love, which is the condition of freedom, leads to the rather astounding picture of world evolution described above. But rather than an absorption of all sentient beings into a unitary Buddha nature, or the ascension of the faithful into a Paradise dominated by the ineffable presence of Allah, the condition of pure conversation, which is essentially a moral, or Judeo-Christian condition, is marked by a different aim. This democratic and Judeo-Christian version of the social organism is a condition of self-made spirits (egos) floating around in material nature (the sense world) and transforming it into a condition approximating their own supersensible will. By concerted but magically coordinated efforts, these spirits (a.k.a. human beings) produce out of the world a Work of self-radiant beauty, mystery and cosmological meaning that can only be grasped in conceptual form by the clairvoyant vision of higher dimensions. Thus,

HypSoc2.1: Hypothesis on future earth evolution.

Given this picture of what pure conversation is ultimately about, we do well to make a careful analysis of how Kant derives the practice of freedom, which is what all future evolution must consist in, from *the conception of natural law*. We must also clearly understand the relationship between freedom and power, which is a related concept. Both law and power must be circumscribed and defined by any theory of conversation. What is the natural law, and not merely the conventional or man-made rule, of conversational action? What natural law, for example, would pertain to a world of egos dependent on their bodies but capable of substantial action outside of them? What would power such a condition? What *power relations* obtain in pure conversation?

Law in General

All of nature, says Kant, functions in accordance with *law*. That is simply what nature is. It is a domain of effects which proceed with universal regularity from well-defined causes. The human being, by way of contrast, functions in accordance with the *conception of law*. He (she) is sensitive to law but is not under its direct dominion. He (she) has one foot in the world of nature, or mechanical and bottom-up effects, and the other in a supersensible domain of ends, or self-sufficient causes, of which he (she) himself (herself), because of his (her) rationality, is one such exemplar.

What is the connection? Where or how do the two domains meet, the realm of thought or conception of law, and the realm of law itself? Kant's answer is that they become identical under a form of thought that directs or commands the will *categorically*. Kant described a form of mental activity in which the mind is brought to a determination of a possible action without having any alternative. Paradoxically, Kant finds the position under the *categorical imperative* to be one in which the will is maximally free, and not, as one might unreflectively imagine, in a condition of mere enslavement. Under this condition, the will is *free to* act in a certain otherwise impossible way, and not merely *free from* certain constraints, conditions or laws. As a principle illustration of this condition, he used the example of duty.

Now the logic of duty is, as the logic of anything is, a matter of its form. Notwithstanding its apparent compulsion and blind indifference, the form and essence of duty is in its *universality*. Without exception, duty requires conformity to its direction. Duty is the directive to which anyone, no matter whom, if placed relevantly under its edict, will respond in an identical manner. Universality is the law of duty. Kant's logic appears to be that experience under a universally binding directive is fundamentally free not because of the directive, which admittedly constrains the will, but because of the structure intrinsic to something universal.

Conversation theory describes a form of *functional universality*, and as such represents a version of the categorical imperative. It describes a condition in which everyone present, regardless of his (her) linguistic (rational) capacities, is fully recognized and completely satisfied at every conversational moment. Under such conditions, the individual speaker can only select a propositional content that he (she) believes is a universal law. Under such conditions, the individual interpreter can only try to understand the propositional content he (she) has just heard as an actual law. Under these conditions, everyone present is functioning as a literal force of nature. Thus,

> HypPhy2: Hypothesis of functional universality (theory of the good will as physical law).

The structure of the physical space under these conditions is really something quite marvelous. Dimensions are added to the three dimensions of the external space in virtue of the openings and closings of the internal spaces of the living bodies. Consciousness, including intuition and emotion, which is carried wave-like in these spaces, is expanded as a result, in the manner of a psychedelic or mystical experience. Under these conditions, the expansion of consciousness is entirely benign, often very subtle, but always causally potent, because there is no way to push the experience past the comfort level of the least adept and the least adventurous.

The added dimensionality of such spatial experience is generally classified as *etheric*, and is a direct consequence of a universally constituted will. The etheric body of occult literature is a *geometrically universal body*, a periphery-centered body, occupying the adjacent level above the physical body, which bears universal features in its own, point-centered way. The etheric body originates in planar gravitational forces pressing inwardly, centripetally, from enormous distances. All of life, we will probably discover, and conditions inside the sun as well, depend on these forces. This "body," if body it truly be, can probably be fully described by a geometry that uses points, lines, planes and solid objects placed at infinity. Universality, which has a geometric interpretation, and as such is a form of natural law, is subtended by infinity.

With such a picture, it is intuitively clear why universality as law should represent freedom to individual experience. Anything that makes direct reference to infinity is going to give an otherwise finite consciousness a glimpse of *glory*, and glory is a form of freedom or power. What else could it be? Anything making a claim on universality makes a claim on infinity, and thus makes a claim on freedom.

Power

To the point-centered egoic consciousness of the common world, power is a form of freedom. To have power over someone or something is, at a minimum, to be free with respect to that person or thing. Power relations in general also confer freedom, and not only to the top dog. If I find myself in a weaker social position with respect to someone or something, I actually gain a certain freedom because I gain a certain *deontic status*. By being in a power relationship (by being Donald Trump's secretary, for example), I have certain circumscribed rights and duties, and a certain number of freedoms pertaining to those rights and duties. I may be less free than King Donald himself, and generally subservient to his will, but I have a little dukedom of my own.

Status functions in general are the key to understanding political freedom, the power of sovereignty and social contract theory, which goes back to Thomas Hobbes in seventeenth-century England. The socialized man is more free than the man in a state of nature, despite the fact that he is more obligated. He has more powers, more things he can do, because he can draw on his status in a social or political body, and thus, for example, build a steel bridge over a wide river, or hire an airplane to fly him into (and out of) a rain forest. A person without social status cannot do these things, and in general can do many fewer things.

Searle's analysis of deontic power has the following form:

(1) X counts as Y in context C;
(2) Society accepts (Y has power (Y does A))

where X is some physical token, such as a dollar bill, Y is the status function, in this case $1 in U.S. currency, and C is the context in which the status is legitimated, in this case the investment, banking and commercial system of the United States of America. Finally, A is an action that Y can or actually does perform. In this case, A would be the purchase of $1 worth of goods or services.

In general, a status function is called an *institution*. Status is a social construction, collectively intended or willed. It exists because human beings collectively intend it to exist. Examples include government, money, family, language and even, I think, truth, goodness and certain aspects of God.

The thing to notice here is that when society accepts the power of some status function or institution, it accepts a certain autonomy in that function or institution. The institution takes on a life of its own. In some sense, accepting the power of an institution is accepting it as a living entity. In some institutions the principle is plainer than in others, for example in the autonomy of the United States Government, or to take an example on a different level, in some of the words spoken by Abraham Lincoln. Some American families, on the other hand, do not appear to have much to recommend them at all as living entities.

Now the remarkable fact is that by conferring autonomy and life on abstract entities such as governments, currencies, families, words or sentences, we reciprocally confer autonomy and freedom on ourselves. The human being becomes more free (capable of more actions) by collectively granting a living power, autonomy or right of action to something other than himself (herself). I think this amounts to some kind of Divinity Principle. As conversational (social) beings, we exercise the life-giving functions of creation, organization and dissolution that are traditionally proper to God and the hierarchies of spirits believed to pervade the cosmic spaces before birth, during life and after death. We do this by collectively conferring status or power upon abstract (conceptual) entities. Call this:

> CCDiv1.0: Divinity principle (principle of authentic collective intentionality).

The divinity principle is a clear challenge to conversation as it is practiced in the current epoch. It requires us, in essence, to act as if we were gods, or better, as if we were angels under the sovereignty of a single God, with all of the status, dignity and power proper to that supersensible realm. Pure conversation, as I am defining it here, and as nearly as I can figure it, is the key to a self-conscious response to the divinity principle.

Pure conversation, with its principles of collective intentionality, transparency and mutual respect and dignity is the modern form of spiritual initiation. Far from making one individual free and powerful above all others, and thereby ordering society in the manner of the ancient civilizations, modern initiation is about making all individuals free and powerful in themselves by requiring them to function in a rigorously social manner. In ancient civilizations, the cosmos made itself felt through the status of a few cold priests and a warlike king. In the civilization of the future, the cosmos will be felt through the status functions produced by rational individuals trying to express their innate and supersensible genius in a purely social modality.

It needs to be emphasized that in pure conversation, which is a purely social circumstance, there are *no power relations* between and among individuals. In pure conversation, everyone is *equally free* (equally powerful). Even when a person possesses a lesser capacity for intelligent judgment or intelligent expression, he (she) retains no less (and no more) freedom of action than the others present. This is a matter of social contract. Pure conversation always functions at the level of the least intelligent individual. In pure conversation, no one is tacitly excluded because of a lesser capacity for freedom or a lesser power of imagination or expression. Call this:

> CCDir1.3: Principle of equal power (principle of the least intelligent).

Chapter 6
ENERGY

Energy is eternal delight —WILLIAM BLAKE

THE ENTIRE POINT of pure conversation is to work with and even to control the cosmo-mechanical energy intrinsic to human consciousness. This "work" is a training to bring the lower energies of habit, of selfishness and of the general lack of self-conscious intelligence under the distributed control of higher moral and practical energy and intelligence. These higher energies and intelligences are subtle and immeasurably real, but are not well understood outside religious contexts. Conversation theory purports to be the general method whereby the phenomena of religious experience can be studied experimentally and positivistically.

Continuity

The basic principle of energy work is *continuity of energy in consciousness*, although there do exist apparent exceptions. The first stage of a real continuity of consciousness or energy, after the development of a basic capacity for conversation, is a transformed dream life that begins to be more and more reflected in waking experiences, and vice versa. At that point, it can be expected that a real capacity for pure conversation has developed. Call this:

NLPhy2.0: Law of the waking dream (continuity of consciousness).

In conversation, the continuity of energy is maintained from the initiation of the conversation, through the play of meanings, until the final sealing, and then is carried as an invisible seed into the world and perhaps back again. This is the basic formula for *conversational alchemy.* Ultimately the continuity of consciousness is presumed somehow to extend beyond death and into a realm of spiritual causes. Future lives are the ultimate destination of the seeds of conversation.

The *logos* of pure conversation, of course, is to operate on or with these spiritual causes during the sojourn in the sense world. Conversation is largely a matter of sensible intuition, taking its cues from subtle indications in the environment, but it is also a matter of the good will, which transcends the sense world. Finding exactly the right content and expressing it in exactly the right way (i.e. in the way that everyone present can accept) calls for powers (energies) that extend beyond ordinary experience. A continuity of conscious energy, which is an extension of the living will, and of logical concatenation, which is essentially, I think, a matter of social formality, is the way to exercise this intuitive capacity for the *logos*. Let us say:

CCSIn1.0: Principle of continuity.
CCSIn1.1: Principle of alchemy

It is important to appreciate, at least as a hypothetical, that the body continuously emits sounds from the joints of its skeleton, and from other internal mechanical causes, such as the heart. These sounds can be intuited in states of inner stillness, and they are probably the necessary gate to the *logos* of conversation. They are the energetic content of the human body. These sono-mechanical resonances are probably also key to the continuity of consciousness. They are the energies associated with the "counterspace" of the living body, the dimensions of space that extend beyond the domain of three dimensions we normally accept as consensual reality. Thus,

HypPsy6.0: Hypothesis on inner sound.

Ineffability

In general, the individual's capacity to circulate, conduct or otherwise maintain a continuity of energy in consciousness varies according to some rather imponderable factors. Certainly diet is a factor in the disposition one brings to a conversation. Also important are sexual interest and hormone levels in the blood. More important is preparedness and one's overall spiritual condition. But other factors, including cosmic factors, also appear to be a real factor in one's dispositionality. The time of the day, the phase of the moon and probably the disposition of other planets and fixed stars all have a bearing on the mood of conversation. Let us say:

> NLPsy6.0: The imponderability of mood (law of dispositionality).

Beyond the vagaries of its ultimate uncontrollability, the dispositionality of energy is important for another reason. Real spiritual experience never repeats itself. Spiritual contents are always one of a kind, and completely specific and sharply defined, and often so surprising that it may take days, years or centuries to understand them. Once experienced or accomplished, they are over with. An event, for example in Palestine, serves as a demonstration for all places and all times. The cosmos has its say, and then moves on.

Such a situation might suggest there is no hope for a scientific treatment, which requires reproducibility both of experimental protocol and of experimental result. Just how serious a limitation this fact about self-conscious contents and self-conscious energy in conversation will prove to be remains to be seen, but the distinction between specific contents and the measurable indicators that must correlate with them may be a distinction between token and type, the latter being objectively describable. Alternatively, using mathematical approaches, it may be possible to show that although these contents actually are specific and numerically distinct brain states, impossible to reproduce in real time because of their sheer complexity, other avenues to understand them may remain open. It may prove possible, given the right instrumentation, to image these states, or reproduce them in a digitized, second order of reality, in the manner of a PET scan or a thermal spectrum. Let us say:

> NLIn2.0: Ineffability condition (first-order moments in the *logos* are absolutely unique).

The ineffability condition on the contents of consciousness has another consequence that must not be overlooked for the sake of realistic expectations in conversation. Once the energy of the conversational moment has passed, it cannot be reconstructed. This may seem to be at odds with the general principle of reproduction, but it is not. Reproduction aims at the form of the current content. No conversational moment is over until its reproduction (its comprehension) is complete. The reproduction phase can be extended indefinitely, through a large number of formal reiterations, because it does nothing to alter the energy quantum of the moment. Such extended reproduction is simply a matter of finishing or trying to finish a conversational moment.

The conversational moment is analogous to the discharge of a battery or capacitor. Once the discharge has been effected, the moment is basically finished. It may be that one could have wished for more from the exchange, that one's professed satisfaction was merely nominal, but one cannot expect superficial perfection in all exchanges. It is simply a fact that with spiritual contents, everything, even the entire cosmos, is given in the moment. The only possible attitude to adopt, if one feels dissatisfied at some inarticulate level with what has just occurred, is to condense the energy of what has been given to seed form, and silently to store it, in the manner of a magician, with the knowledge that its complete unfolding is inevitable. Let us say:

NLPhy3.0: Law of spiritual discharge (capacitor principle);
CCSIn1.2: Principle of silent work (seed principle).

Fields

It needs to be understood that with pure conversation, we are exercising a *field phenomenon*, a radiation or flux from individual bodies and minds of undetermined composition. The field no doubt is quite complex, involving the global interaction of individualities with fields of varying capacities. These individual fields undoubtedly add together and cancel out, presumably in lawlike ways. The physical medium of the field of conversation is probably both electromagnetic and sono-mechanical. Gravitational and harmonic effects are also present. Beyond these, in terms of a rigorous physical theory, I prefer not to speculate. Let us say:

NLPhy4.0: Principle of the physical field.

On the other hand, a number of qualitative descriptors of the physical field can be usefully detailed. In the first instance, the etheric field has buoyant qualities, as though it represents a form of anti-gravity. These buoyant forces can, at times, seem strong enough subjectively to levitate masses physically, although it is doubtful that physical levitation can objectively occur. It may be, on the other hand, that the so-called out-of-body experience, in which consciousness appears to be projected above, beyond or outside the confines of normal physical space, is caused by this levitational field. Let us say:

NLPhy5.0: Levitation.

Intensive breathing combined with specific postural alignments, as practiced in yoga and the martial arts can lead to other configurations of this etheric force. The basic configurations, described by spiritual and martial adepts who can be presumed to know about them are: *up and down, center to periphery* and *spirals*. These directions or vectors can occur both inside and outside the physical body. Such is the esoteric anatomy of the human energy system.

These purported energy circulations, which are powered by the interaction of mind, breath and posture, are fiendishly difficult to control, and hence to exploit for whatever purpose one may have. On the other hand, if I am correct about their proper place and function in the cosmos, and about their true or ultimate cause, a well-behaved use of language (i.e. a well-formed conversation) can release these archetypal circulations and render them, together with their levitational or projective qualities, a matter of common experience and daily life. Such experience can devolve only from a high human culture embracing the whole of human history, human knowledge and human tradition, together with an objective understanding of its errors and its glories. I believe conversation theory is the only possible foundation for this culture.

Another feature of the human energy circulation needs to be understood. This is the *purifying effect* that such circulation has on the mind and the body. The Catholic Mass, for example, is used to wash the blood and emotions of the faithful. Confession, for psychological reasons, has similar effects. Yogic breathing techniques, particularly if embedded in the right ritual, have effects that, at a minimum, effect this internal purification. Priestly and magical rituals purport to do more than merely to purify, and perhaps they do, but the experience of purification is commonplace enough to be more or less incontrovertible. What the precise mechanism of inner purification actually is, entailing an interaction between the etheric body, the higher astral body and the blood, I will not speculate about here. Suffice it to say:

NLPhy5.1: Up to down, down to up;
NL5.2: Center to periphery, periphery to center;
NL5.3: Spirals;
NLPsy7.0: Etheric purity and purification.

Although the *yoga of breath* is an unexceptionable method to convince anyone of the reality of the transcendental circulations of energy, and of their physical power, it is not the yogic method of the future. The yoga of the future is a *yoga of light*, a moral and social yoga grounded in the rigors of conversation theory. This approach alone has the potential for any sort of progressive evolution of human life on earth. It is aimed, moreover, at the ultimate and true cause of all circulations of bodily and mental energy. It is aimed at the human ego, which purportedly circulates through the cosmos from lifetime to lifetime in a great Play of self-realization and the transcendence of karmic error. The projective geometries of space, the harmonic octaves of sound and resonance, the purifying energies of universal truth, the ideal forms resting at and descending from infinity are the cognitive tools of this great yoga. These are the proper content and focus of the human social life, and the real cause and motive of all conversation.

The human energy circulation is probably traceable to a single mechanism: *physical resonance*. The human body is assembled around a number of oscillators and polarities – the heart and blood circulation, the nervous discharge, the muscle contraction, the cranio-sacral polarity, the digestive cycle, sleep and wakefulness, sexual interest and disinterest. By physical necessity, each of these cycles or rhythms radiates waves of energy in various media, and these waves interact in textbook ways that are physically well-understood. What is not at all understood is what these waves and types of wave *add up to* in the case of a whole individual or a whole society of individuals. That is simply an unexplored mystery.

I believe that the sum of all resonances in the human body in large part is language, and the consciousness of the *logos* that makes language an absolute necessity for the human ego. I believe it is the *meaning* of the intended linguistic act, and as such is the *reference* of that act. All acts of meaning are tied causally to physical objects and historical situations. That is the causal theory of reference. The mystery is that the reference (i.e. the physical extension) of any locution or thought, which is materially real, is itself nothing but a bundle of resonances. This is what the atomic theory of matter says. But then linguistic reference, which is itself a pattern of resonance in the human body, has no more and no less ultimate significance than those other patterns of resonance called physical objects extended beyond it in space and time. Who is to say which cause has ultimate priority? Let us say,

> HypPhy4.0: Hypothesis on materiality (thought is sufficient for matter).

On top of the mystery of resonance and the ultimate materiality of nature stands the beauty and the glory of the harmonics of all wave energies, and their role in the human energy system. The musical octave, as astounding a product of natural law and natural selection as any product of cosmic evolution can be is probably a force hidden in the form and function of the human body itself. Indeed, to reiterate the mystery, cosmic evolution may somehow be a product of musical and luminary octaves, and not the other way around. Conversation at any rate, if it is to be turned to its full and lawful potential, will certainly prove to be a musical affair. Energetic bliss, the eternal delight of the mystic and the meditator, is certainly a result of the harmonies intrinsic to human energy being freed and allowed to have their way. Thus,

HypPhy4.1: Hypothesis on bliss (bliss is wave harmonics).

The Cosmos

It should be understood that in this essay the term "cosmic" refers to very commonplace phenomena that are today, in our fascination with our success with economics and engineering, ignored as objects of reverence and awe. This trend must be reversed if we are to institute conversation in its true form. Night and day, the phases of the moon, the weather, the tides, earthquakes and volcanoes and the seasons are all literal cosmic phenomena. That the human being participates on this scale seems an incontrovertible fact. In all probability, birth and death, speech and language, waking, sleeping and dreaming, society and sex are best understood and experienced as cosmic phenomena. Conversation in the sense I am defining it here must certainly be understood and experienced in this way.

Orientation of direction is a basic *a priori* condition on conversation. The north-south axis is a basic conversational condition, and a cosmic one at that. It probably makes some sort of difference in conversation which way certain individuals are oriented on the surface of the earth. Changing these orientations during the conversation in a controlled manner is one way to test for this cosmic effect. Physical displacement or substitution of individuals is another way. Tracing signs and sigils over the surface of the earth (a cosmic dimension) is yet another. For example, a conversational concatenation can proceed, by prior agreement, from individual to individual placed in the form of a pentagram. Very definite energetic effects can be elicited in this manner. Why these effects occur and what they signify can only await some kind of scientifically informed consensus.

CCST2.1: Principle of spatial orientation.

The human voice is probably best regarded as a cosmic phenomenon. The energy that radiates from the human voice has the power to cause specific responses in the energy system of those who attend to it. The content of what is spoken has a further such power. In common social intercourse these two effects are taken together and treated as one, but as a practical and experimental matter, they are separate and separable functions. To control this play of semanto-mechanical energy, we need cooperatively to make of it both a science and a high form of culture.

Proper speech is fundamental to this sort of program. The human voice and larynx should be deployed to their maximum effect, in the manner of drama or oratory. Rhythm, intonation, articulation, projection and modulation can all be exercised and developed as objective capacities. When combined with a cultural expectation of the *logos* in the content of all speech, the result can be otherworldly. Under such conditions, it is as if the spell of the magician were deployed and distributed throughout the entire social body, causing each body to be buoyed into an etheric world existing in a dimension coincident with the dimensions of the common world, but little noticed or understood by the common consciousness. Let us say:

NLPhy6.0: Principle of reciprocal causality (everybody affects everybody else energetically just by being present).

The clairvoyant philosopher of the age, Rudolf Steiner, indicated that in the distant, but not unforeseeably distant future, the human being would begin to reproduce its kind by means of the speech and the larynx. The organs of reproduction in the future would be much higher up in the body, and of a purified nature. Women would cease to bear the young, and the fascination of the genitals would be replaced by a general reverence and regard for the forms of nature. Man would have ascended into an etheric domain, the realm of pure cosmic energy and ongoing delight. The reproductive technique of pure conversation, which is the essence of the *logos*, would become the reproductive impulse of the entire species.

As a matter of fact, all manner of human movement, gesture, speech and thought are cosmic movements, with all of the potential for beauty, grandeur and awesome dignity that this status would imply. The problem of conscious evolution is to get people to act as if this potential were something they could or should take seriously. The subtlety of becoming a literal and continuous force of nature and the cosmos is something people are not in general adapted to take on. Yet I think this unpreparedness is not in general a matter of their irresponsibility. The cause of our cosmically impoverished souls lies outside of us, in the cultural and educational influences which work into us in numberless ways. We are products of a cultural epoch, and the current epoch is about material mastery and economic maximization. With conversation theory, however, we have a way to reconstruct our values and cultural matrix along lines that are more cosmically correct.

The correct way to move, to speak and to think is in such a way that the energy of the human system is circulated pleasurably from each of the many hundreds of spaces and points inside and outside the body in a continuous manner. The affair is very complex, requiring a great deal of strength and moral will to practice effectively, but I believe it can be made an entirely natural part of growing into adulthood if our cultural values and expectations are gradually altered in the right way. We should insure that it is always possible, on a few moments notice, for an individual to discover the precise content (the actual *logos*) that allows his (her) energy to circulate freely. With that experience institutionalized, the individual is then committed to *build on* what he (she) has learned about himself and the world in which he (she) lives. The City of God, one remembers from St. John, is built from heaven downward, and not in the usual terrestrial way. Let us say:

HypSoc2.2: Idea of cosmic construction.

Emotional Requirements

In addition to the physical principles above, cosmic conversation theory requires a series of emotional principles. These principles are relevant not to the etheric body, which is essentially gravitational (or anti-gravitational), but to the astral body, which is truly cosmic and spacious. The leading emotional principle is:

> CCSIn2.1: Principle of equanimity (sit still and stay re-laxed).

This has more than one meaning, but everything emotional is in it. Outward stillness, if it is a relaxed stillness, is sufficient to accommodate the entire range of emotional experience. I do not see how real conversations can be conducted on any other institutional basis. If the personality is allowed to dominate the energy of conversation, only degenerate forms can result.

A second emotional principle is positivity. This may seem to be unbalanced, but in principle negativity has no place in conversation. The law of antipathy (NL5) is more than adequate to ensure a healthy dose of negative energy in any conversation. There is no justification for institutionalizing it. Authentic positivity, on the other hand, is such a rare commodity in most social intercourse that we do well to enshrine it as a principle. In fact it is logically necessary to do so. The good will must continually be put on display if a truly social circumstance is to succeed. The will, which is generally sound asleep in the point-centered, gravity-bound human being, needs routine exercise and correction if it is to become a cosmic force. The yoga of the future simply requires the exhibition of positive thoughts and gestures by all members of the social body. The technique has several variations, the most accessible perhaps being the "Yes, and..." technique of improvised theater. Here the several players, having no specific knowledge of what is going to occur next on the stage, can be ready only to express a total acceptance of and commitment to whatever one of their fellows does or says for everyone to witness. Such a technique is absolutely necessary to keep an improvised scene alive on stage. Let us say:

CCSIn2.2: Principle of positivity.

A third emotional principle is open-mindedness. This is the key to an imagination that can be controlled and utilized directly in the construction of an artificial etheric realm. The process of cosmic creation is by no means at an end. Indeed, now that things have cooled considerably, and in a way are beginning to die, an extrusive phase is beginning. Human activity itself contains the laws of this phase of cosmic and earth evolution. Under these conditions, the conversational human being must be able to think to himself (herself), sometimes in the face of something utterly absurd, "What if this were really true?" Let us say:

CCSIn2.3: Principle of open-mindedness.

The Schematism

The essence of conversational energy can perhaps be captured by a finite series of conversational *schemata*. Kant appears to have believed as much, and in his first Critique he was at pains to describe a schematism of the categories of the individual's egoic understanding. For example, reality, he decided, is recognized in everyone's understanding as a primitive gesture or schema in the mind he described as "a continuous and uniform production of a quantity in time as we successively descend from a sensation which has a certain degree to its vanishing point, or progressively ascend from its negation to some magnitude of it." Perhaps there really is such a schematism in the conversational spirit. Perhaps we will learn to recognize it consensually. Thus,

HypPsy8.0: Hypothesis on the schematism.

I am generally sympathetic to an approach that conceives consciousness as fundamentally a function of *posture*, or internal and external bodily alignments that conduce toward the circulation of psychic energy. That is the theoretical picture of conversation – individuals with good self control and at the same time willing and able to move to a new "posture," mechanically induced and objectively describable, in response to ordered changes in the fields of others. On this picture, conversation is really a physical mechanism. It is a matrix of energy and mechanicality that coincides with movements in the energy and mechanics of the cosmos itself. Thus,

CCArtSC2.0: Principle of good posture.

Chapter 7

INTENTIONALITY

Love under Will is the Law. —ALEISTER CROWLEY

IN GENERAL, THE only reason to hold a conversation is to create a work of art. For other purposes, such as deciding how to meet an organization's current budget shortfall, lesser forms of social intercourse will do. But holding a conversation is something special. It is an exercise of something that, though deprived of all sensible reference and sensible motive, would nevertheless of itself sparkle like a valuable jewel in the space where it was conceived and executed. This "something" is the good will, and Kant calls it the *only thing in this world* that can be thought of as *good without qualification*.

Accordingly, intentionality or will is something that needs to be understood by every conversationist. Recent analytic philosophy has produced a precise and refined picture of the conditions necessary for intentionality, intentional actions and meaning intentions. It is not essential to have a total technical grasp of the logic of intentionality in order to sustain pure conversation, but I think it is important to wrestle with it a little bit in advance. That wrestling, after all, is what will happen in real time during each conversation. Practice makes perfect.

Intentions are, above all, self-referential. They are themselves the entities which satisfy the reference they make. Now we know, from the causal theory of reference, that all reference stands in a causal relation to the things or situations in the world to which it refers. Intentions therefore cause or are caused by the conditions which satisfy them.

Suppose I try (intend) to cross my legs. The content in my mind is therefore:

(1) This intention causes (my legs cross)
      A   B

where the first part (A) is a living state of self-conscious activity in me and the second part (B) is the condition that satisfies that living state. The actual action of my legs crossing *refers* to an intention somewhere in space, in this case to (1), that causes that action. Reference is very much an objective feature of the world.

Now suppose I have electrodes implanted in my motor cortex, and these cause my legs to be crossed in robot fashion. In this case, something is missing. Here, my legs crossing *has no reference*. Their crossing is essentially meaningless. The movement occurs in the soulless manner of a machine.

Suppose I receive an impression of a painting (suppose I look at a painting). The content in my mind is:

(2) This painting causes (I have this visual impression).
      A   B

Here the direction of causation is reversed. In this case, B and not A is the intentional state, a perceptual state, and A, not B, is the condition which satisfies the state. The existence of the painting in that particular aspect refers to an intention, in this case (2), somewhere in space that is caused by that existence.

Now suppose I have electrodes implanted in my visual cortex that cause me apparently to see the painting. In this case again, something is missing, namely the real existence of a painting in causal relationship with the perceptual state. Such an experience, if it were taken seriously, would, like a virtual reality game, be so solipsistic as to be essentially meaningless.

So both actions and perceptions are intentionalistic. In conversation, both efforts to speak and efforts to understand are self-referential and causally linked to things (energies) in the world. Now, for the purposes of insuring a general good will, which is the essence of real conversation, those efforts need to be linked to things and situations of the highest and noblest order to which the human being is capable of making reference. These efforts need to be *inspired* efforts. Nothing less will do.

This condition, call it:

CCSIn3.0: Principle of inspiration,

is nothing more and nothing less than the requirement that every effort at conversational speech and every effort at conversational comprehension needs to aim at a content that is *beyond what has been articulated so far*. Each such effort needs to be causally linked to a heretofore supersensible (inarticulate) content of universal importance in such a way that that content makes itself felt, by means of causal reference, in the real time of the conversation. For real conversation, nothing less will suffice. Call this:

CCSIn3.1: Principle of the super-effort (principle of pure intentionality).

Basically what is occurring under conditions of pure intentionality (pure conversation) is that a content is being located that both satisfies the speech intention of the token conversationist, indifferently selected, and that satisfies the perception that each conversationist has in that conversational moment. It is a matter of both causal directions occurring in the same conversational moment. This *double direction of causation* is the general structure of inspired speech. Sexual orgasm, magical invocation, inspired rhetoric and ecstasy in general are examples of this double direction of causation. Small wonder that levitational effects can follow from pure conversation; small wonder that divinity is the proper destiny of well-formed social exchanges and the spaces in which they occur!

Anthroposophical Content and Hegel's Dialectic

What manner of content can possibly suffice for this condition of ecstasy to be satisfied in democratic social circumstances? The answer in general, I think, is *anthroposophical* content. It is the kind of content developed by the clairvoyant philosopher Rudolf Steiner in his Goethean-Kantian demonstration of the human potential for direct knowledge of the higher spiritual worlds. It is the content hinted at in the Platonic dialogs and in the entire Western philosophical tradition, when that tradition has been handled by its best exemplars in their best moments, from Aristotle to Spinoza, from Aquinas to Heidegger. It is a content that views Man as the primary and fundamental law of nature, and sees the cosmos and all of natural law as focussed on the creation and production of the moral force intrinsic to rational human conduct. It is, moreover, a content that finds it sufficient to understand the impulses and practices of God consciousness, provided that understanding is clairvoyant, and not blindly to accept them in the manner of guru-devotion, faith or zealous commitment.

In a sense, the anthroposophical principle is *Hegel's dialectic* applied to moral conduct, the social contract and the individual's manner of life. It is the principle which says, "Every human being has its logic and therefore its validity; every person, whatever his (her) mental state and mental commitments, is a person of worth and substance; every cultural development, every personal philosophy, every actual point of view is a real and rational manifestation of the cosmos itself. But there is an objective *progression and hierarchy of reason.* There is an intentionality or will both in reason and in evolution itself. Some manifestations of the cosmos take place on higher levels, some on lower ones. To understand and articulate the higher ones, it is necessary to understand and articulate the lower ones. The value, substance and reality of the individual, and of the particular culture, whatever it may be, *fits somewhere* in a gigantic scheme and impulse (intention) to build God's Eternal City on Earth." Call this:

CCAn1.0: Principle of anthroposophical teleology (principle of Hegel's dialectic).

The anthroposophical principle has another aspect. To put it simply, it says that the proper and complete expression (understanding) of some mental content is equivalent to, or just as good as, the possession of that content itself. Thus, if one can understand the concept of spiritual enlightenment, one is in some sense already enlightened. If one can understand and fully express the concept of karma, one already possesses, in some sense, the reality of one's past lives. If one can fully express the concept of the etheric body, one's etheric body will be aroused and revealed.

The conversational entailments here are deep. Only philosophical and anthroposophical contents will do for the purposes of real conversation: God in general; karma in general; the will in general; enlightenment, thought, freedom, power, and morality in general; the cosmic harmonies, the evolution of man, the social contract, and the sexes in general; Christ, Abraham, Mohammad, the Buddha, China, the Vedas, the Middle Ages, America; technology in general, DNA in general, information in general and so forth. Particular contents will not do: business, professional sports, personal psychology, today's weather, personal reminiscence, political agendas and so forth. In general, if conversation (universal satisfaction) about mental contents can be sustained, and if those mental contents have some cosmic significance, then those contents will become largely linked to their actual reference, and everybody will both know it and will be put into a position to use that actual condition for his (her) own development. Call this:

> CCAn1.1: The anthroposophical principle (principle of the spiritual intellect).

The Intentionality of Conversation

Now it is important to recognize that the will in most of us is sound asleep, and in cases where it is awake or partially awake, as it is in individuals capable of high performance, such as superior athletes or driven entrepreneurs, it is usually incompletely or even wrongly developed. A properly developed will is capable of clairvoyant intuition, and not only that, but clairvoyance of a sort that is socially well-adjusted. A socially adjusted clairvoyance is not only enlightened, and thus free of all dependence on tutelage of any sort, but responsible to a certain degree for that sector of society and social relations to which it is committed. A properly developed will is at any moment both free and comfortable in and with the body, because in a way it *sees through it*, and free and comfortable in the presence of any and all others, whatever their social status may be, because likewise it *sees through them*.

The great obstacle to the god-like will, to the will that commands the etheric body as readily as it does the physical body, is fantasy and the common imagination. This is the mechanism in the human body that is responsible for the "monkey mind" of the meditator, for the difficulty most people have with a sustained and total concentration of the mind and body, and for the degenerate nature of conversation as it commonly occurs in today's world. It is the wandering attention, the tendency to be taken and absorbed by a "buffer" in the mind, which is probably nothing more and nothing less than the brain itself, with its incalculable capacity for intelligent activity. Such an instrument placed in an underdeveloped social and cultural circumstance is almost certain to waste its potential in useless and circular machinations. Call this,

> CCSIn4.0: Principle of the imagination (principle of fantasy).

A properly awakened will is not a matter of brain gyrations at all; rather, it is a matter of an awakened spinal column, with its more or less direct connectivity to the soft and hollow organs, to the blood circulation and to the joints and limbs. The spine is the key to a comfortable circulation in the body, and to an etheric circulation in conversation. Call this:

> NLPhy7.0: The spinal-mechanical principle (principle of the will).

What then are the conditions of satisfaction of a will (an intentionality) under the conditions of pure conversation? At a minimum, they are a comfortable whole bodily sensation, as though one were floating in warm water. Variations on the theme are possible of course, but in general:

(3) This intention causes (my body remains comfortable).

Of course, the trick is now to add linguistic (rational) intentions on top of this. What about the enormous ganglion on top of the spinal column? What does *it* do during a good conversation?

The present theory is an attempt to answer that question, and the basic answer is that the brain must intend simultaneously to satisfy all of the conditions of pure conversation with sensory and cognitive clarity. In essence, however, I think the intentionality of the brain in pure conversation comes to this:

(4) This intention causes (I create a work of art).

Art is the expression of something universal (something cosmic) in a medium. That something universal, of course, is the thought, intuition or content that the speaker proposes everyone present accept as truth. And of course, because of the tonalities and gestures of the medium in which it is expressed, that content is in significant part the speaker himself (herself). So the intention is actually:

(5) This intention causes (I am a work of art).

Now the extreme self-consciousness entailed by this sort of intention is either radically mitigated or excruciatingly amplified by the perceptual half of the conversational moment:

(6) This work of art causes (everyone receives this impression).

If the art (artifice) is successful, everyone warmly accepts it as real and actual, and likewise the speaker's self-consciousness surfaces as a gentle warming from the inside; if it is insincere, half-baked or otherwise fumbled, someone will express dissatisfaction. Depending on who and how, this exception can be embarrassing, even painful. But painful embarrassment can be remedial, even salutary, and in any case, the process of reproductive specification must now, by the fundamental conversational algorithm, begin. In any case, the self-consciousness of ordinary embarrassment is transformed by good conversation into a spiritual self-consciousness that simply transcends the judgments, indices and dispositions of ordinary relations. The self-consciousness of pure conversation is like the self-consciousness of the angels: warm, egalitarian, transparent, exact, cooperative and ecstatic.

So the intentionality of pure conversation, from moment to moment is:

(7) This intention causes ((I remain comfortable in my body)
$\wedge$ (my body is a work of art))

and

(8) My body causes (everyone receives an identical impression of the intentionality in my body).

Let us say:

CCArtSC1.0: The principle of self-consciousness (the principle of conversation as art);
CCArtSC1.1 The principle of conversational intentionality (7 and 8 above).

Extra-Conversational Intentionality

There are a number of extra-conversational principles and conditions necessary to develop the will for clairvoyant conversation. One of these is *thinking backwards*. Not only should the conversationist be capable of subtle and extensive logic with respect to conversational contents, and a clear separation of conversational contents from meta-conversational contents, but he (she) should also be capable of a preterlogic, a capacity to reverse, suspend or otherwise invert the current content so that its astral dimension can invade the conversational space. Clairvoyance is precisely a consciousness of this astral dimension, and the capacity to string syllables together in a way that mirrors or reverses their natural progression, the hypnotic power of which generally goes unnoticed in ordinary conversation, is a way to open the astral gate. Variations on this basic thinking exercise exist, and all of these should be practiced by individuals serious about conversation.

For example, suppose during a conversation someone refers to Bill Gates. From the causal theory of reference, we know that the mere mention of the term "Bill Gates" is sufficient to link the conversationists to Bill Gates himself, in one or several of his actual manifestations. It is just a fact about the astral world that the entire energetic impingement of Bill Gates on the conversation can be clarified and focused, and sometimes completely dispelled, by deliberately pronouncing his name backwards, "Setag Llib." Of course this name reversal cannot be executed seriously without the right contextual buildup and the relevant social approval, and the trick will be to find the right way to do so. The principle of reversed names however is a valid one, and at a minimum can be accomplished inwardly and silently, and holds as a general way to exercise thinking. Let us therefore say:

NLPsy8.0: Astral inversion;
CCSIn5.0: The exercise of thinking.

Exercises for the will also exist, and these should be chosen and employed according to temperament and capacity. A simple but difficult exercise recommended by Rudolf Steiner is to set a particular time during the day at which to perform a pointless action, remember to do it and follow through. A good action is to stand in a chair for a minute and a half at some point in the middle of the day. All of the faculties of the sleeping will rebel against such an intention, and one must apply oneself fiercely to accomplish the exercise. Without *strength* in the will, pure conversation is unlikely to flower. Let us say:

CCSIn6.0: The exercise of willing (principle of strength in the will).

These extra-conversational conditions are part of a *basic conversational cycle*, which like conversation proper is a matter of the will. It goes as follows. First there is the conversation, wherein energy is circulated, supersensible impressions are gained and decisions for future actions are taken. Then the conversation is sealed and the cosmic energy, which during the conversation was a matter of free and open conductivity, is cut off. An energetic residue remains, however, both in the space where the conversation took place and in the etheric and astral bodies of the individuals who participated in the conversation. This residue begins to work on its own trajectory in the supersensible domains. It is a supersensible seed.

Gradually what happened during the conversation fades from memory and is forgotten – people sleep, are taken by the exigencies of their lives, pursue their personal interests and inclinations; likewise the world space of the conversation is disused, or perhaps innocently used for some other purpose. Generally speaking, what was in its time a great work of art degenerates and is reduced to a vague shell. Then at some point, it is remembered that *another conversation* is planned for a certain place and time. One begins to look forward to a time of purification, of insight and of development and growth. One begins to prepare oneself and the space, now somewhat sacred, where the conversation will occur. The spiritual seeds of prior conversations, should they see fit to do so, begin to awaken and put out rootlets and buds.

The time of foregathering approaches, and everyone has tuned himself (herself), through concentrated preparation, to a fine intellectual and emotional pitch. It has been decided exactly what the content of the meeting is to be, and that content is challenging to the intellect. One knows that one will be tested and judged by others. Everyone enters the gate and experiences in an entirely new and unexpected way the ecstasy, profundity and rejuvenation of the cosmic circulation. The environmental space in which the conversation occurs similarly undergoes this transformation (that at least is the theory), and the cycle repeats itself.

Schematically, the basic cycle looks like Figure 10. This cycle is both serious and solemn, especially the Entering and Sealing formalities. For reasons that are not well understood, both Entering and Sealing have energetic effects both in the world and subjectively, in the astral and etheric bodies. Magical effects, however, do not justify a wholesale collapse into magical thinking. In fact, it is the essence of

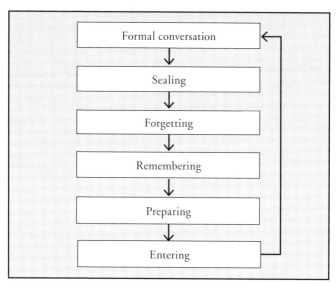

Figure 10: The Basic Conversational Cycle

the conversational will, and of the process of modern spiritual initiation, to keep thought and thinking wholly on the level of material and logical causation while squarely confronted with phenomena and results of a magical and supersensible character. Let us say:

CCArtSC3.0: The basic conversational cycle.

It is altogether reasonable to think of pure and formal conversation as something like a simulation or *simulacrum*, a matrix of reality and experience that is dreamed up out of the collective moral will. The Basic Cycle is the scheme whereby that supersensible matrix is made to interact with the common world of sense and rationality. Pure conversation is a contact point, a node where the two worlds, the sensible and the supersensible, make contact with, enter into and fertilize one another. Needless to say, from the point of view of the denizens of the supersensible worlds, should they be deemed to exist, it may seem that our material existence is the real simulacrum. Most probably, everyone will decide that both domains are real and are each part of a great cosmic polarity of mutual reciprocity and interdependence. Let us say:

CCArtSC4.0: The idea of the simulacrum.

Meaning

A new theory of language must be in essence a new theory of linguistic meaning, and no discussion of conversational intentionality can do without a naturalistic analysis of this crucial and complicated topic. I have described some of the factors in semantic or model theory, and have shown how these dovetail conceptually with the biological notions of fit and satisfaction. Here we need to consider what it is to intend or experience linguistic meaning from a first person point of view, and to make plausible the general conversational hypothesis that meaning thus observed is physical wave resonance and wave energetics.

The first step is to put the neurobiological picture on the table, and the best one is probably Francis Crick (1916–2004) and Cristof Koch's (b. 1956) idea of a *neuronal penumbra* around the neuronal correlate of consciousness. Consciousness, according to these theorists, is turned on by a "winning coalition" of high-level sensory and frontal areas of the cortex, regulated by nuclei in the brainstem, the basal forebrain and the thalamus. On this model, consciousness is largely sensory. Outside of consciousness are other systems of neurons of varying degrees of activity, and linguistic meaning is one of them (another one of them is the sense of "I"). Suppose you are conscious of Bill Clinton. Outside this particular conscious representation is a set of other representations of the man, for example his distinctive voice, his enormous appetite for experience, and his affair with Monica, his partnership with Hillary, many of which may not be consciously represented in the moment, but which "fill out" the conscious experience. On the Crick/Koch model, the *meaning* of "Bill Clinton" gives rise to the *quality* of "Bill Clinton."

From this model we can see the enormous significance of linguistic meaning, insofar as meaning is what makes qualitative human experience possible. From this we can see as well that if Kant is correct, the biological theory of meaning will need to cohere, and perhaps to coincide with the biological theory of rationality, because rationality is, according to Kant, what makes experience or consciousness possible. Remarkably, we have in the general Searlean picture of intentionality, rehearsed above to a degree, a material framework for understanding both meaning and rationality. It seems possible that from this framework we can draw up a *protocol for decomposing and recomposing human experience itself* to produce a modern spiritual initiation of human consciousness using only a well-formed understanding of the elements of experience – of rationality, meaning, intentionality, illocutionary action and the categorical imperative. This protocol will be an applied theory of conversation.

Now it is important to draw attention to the several senses of meaning. These several senses are in themselves enough to confound an intelligible treatment of what meaning fundamentally is, because it is very easy to start by speaking of one and end by speaking of another. Since Frege's predicate calculus, this treatment has become a little more tractable, with the distinction between the sense of a linguistic term or proposition and the reference of that term or proposition, and the development of the crucial concept of the *intension* of a word or phrase, the *index* of a world, a time, a position, an individuality and other such assigned to it. In general, in treating the concept of meaning, one speaks of

1. The meaning (reference) of a name, word or sentence;
2. The meaning (inference) of a logical syllogism or concatenation;
3. The meaning (intension) of a word, phrase or propositional attitude;
4. The meaning (implication) of an act or usage;
5. The meaning (intention) of a speech act;
6. The meaning (significance) of an act, event or situation;
7. The meaning (sense) of a locution or usage;
8. The meaning (designation) of a identifying sign or mark.

Notwithstanding the welter of possibilities contained here, I believe the first-person core of meaning has something to do with the physical energetics and mode of consciousness of the human system. Meaning is a cosmo-mechanical potential in the human being of a very profound *social order*. From our ordinary point of view in space and time this potential gives us the capacity to form *concepts* of objects, events and situations (rules and expectations under which it becomes possible for us to handle those things) that in themselves are wholly transcendent over our ordinary consciousness. Meanings are concepts. Without concepts and the judgment of concepts, there is no human experience, only animal consciousness, and beyond those concepts and judgments, there is psychedelic mystery. Thus:

> HypPhy4.2: The theory of wave functions (the physics of concepts);
> CCMn1.0: The transcendental function of meaning (the condition on the possibility of *qualia*).

There are two basic theories in the mainstream philosophical literature about how the transcendental function of meaning materially takes place, and they are both theories of the free will. These are the *representational* theory, put forward by materialistic thinkers like John Searle, and the *anti-representational* point of view, exemplified best by Donald Davidson (1917–2003), a psychological philosopher of speech and language who believed our reasons for acting are actual causes of our acting. Whether it is correct to say that consciousness *represents* the conditions of satisfaction of its intentionality (including its meaning intentions) is a debate about which I am personally undecided. The view has much to recommend it. The information processing view of cognitive science and neuropsychology, the maxims of action in Kantian moral theory, the probability of a schematism underlying the possibility of all consciousness and all experience, and the commonplace experience of trying to accomplish something difficult with effort all suggest spatial configurations in the brain or astral body that correspond with spatial configurations outside or somehow on the other side of it. Against it, as Davidson pointed out, is the apparently insuperable difficulty of seeing how to prevent a regress of electrochemical or astral schemata corresponding directly not to an outer world, which seems categorically impossible, but merely to some other set of schemata, which seems to be the only thing a schema in general could possibly correspond with. And if meaning can only correspond with other meanings, a wave-functional picture of conceptualization and thought in general makes, on the face of it, a good bit of sense.

For Searle on the other hand, to mean something in general is to impose socially pre-arranged conditions of satisfaction on biologically represented conditions of satisfaction. If I raise my arm to signal the advance of a column of enemy troops, it must be agreed with my interlocutor(s) that the condition that my arm rises (one condition that satisfies my intention to mean something) itself be satisfied by an additional condition. That additional condition is that my interlocutor(s) recognize that my arm rising *represent something conceptual and supersensible*, in this case the *proposition* that the enemy is advancing. The situation thus involves a social or deontic arrangement wherein tokens of intentional behavior *in themselves*, such as raising an arm or uttering certain syllables, are not only intended to materialize, but are also intended to fulfill a certain *deontology*, an obligation that they signify something to anyone who shares a certain social background with the speaker or the signaller.

Now the important psychological or first person sense of meaning in the above list is number six, meaning as signification or significance. Searle's representational analysis can make sense of psychologically meaningful dreams, psychologically meaningful situations and psychologically meaningful relationships as well as of mere meaningful utterances if we assume the required social background is shared at times with a bevy of supersensible beings who are working hard to organize world evolution. Synchronistic events and spiritual dreams, after all, can be quite meaningful. If we remain open-minded here, the question becomes, what is the nature of this common background? What possible community can be discerned between the point-centered existence of material egoity, where our experience by and large takes place, and the periphery-centered existence of cosmic intelligence, where our experience before birth and after death takes place? I think these two different and incommensurable types of intelligence can be conceived to interact under, and only under, the *presupposition of love*, which is clearly a form of pre-arranged unity, and perhaps nothing but an *a priori* and cosmic set of wave functions and wave functional capacities. Outside the domain of love, we can be sure that no intelligent beings exchange any kind of meaningful (conceptual) contents.

The plausibility of this line of argument can perhaps be advanced by considering the meaning communities between ourselves, whose consciousness embraces three dimensions of space and one of time, and our domesticated animals, whose conscious experience is limited to two dimensions of space. These two forms of life are clearly able to exchange meaningful (conceptual) contents, and here again the social presupposition is love. The dog who faithfully guards my property, the horse who transports me to the village and back again, and the goose whom I feed liberally all converse with me on the moral basis of love. Outside the reciprocities, our lives and our experiences are as different as suns and planets. Thus,

> HypPsy7.0: The presupposition of love (the foundation of psychological meaning).

If love is the ultimate pre-arrangement, making all manner of intra- and interspecies communication and conceptual meaning possible, it remains to explain what gives meaning its *resilience*, how the most unloving thoughts and deeds can nevertheless be expressed and communicated within and between life forms. Here I think it is important to appreciate the full range of the deontic background produced by love. If I say,

> (9) Sam is a disgusting drunk

and mean it, not only do I *commit* myself to the truth, sincerity and evidence of this proposition, but I also require of my listener (*direct*) that he (she) accept of Sam that he have this property of being a drunk, and that Sam be saddled with this social status until further notice. All meaningful utterances and signals have this structure. Not only do they impose deontic conditions of satisfaction on their *tokens of intention*, but they also attempt to impose status functions on their *objects of reference*. Love is a very sticky thing.

For this reason, all conversational utterances (conversational meanings) are immediately suspicious and demand careful scrutiny. They are, after all by nature attempts to co-opt, if not to coerce the *political will* of him (her) who interprets them. If a meaningful (conceptual) utterance is accepted conversationally, a host of logical entailments that were previously absent now enter the conversational background as actual, almost legal obligations or commitments. No wonder love is messy! Every conversational act is politically and not merely deontically significant because it has a meaning and hence a *binding power* on the scope, extension and physical energy of the social experience.

In ordinary social relations, of course, this terrible power of love is mitigated by all manner of signs and signals emanating from the heretofore passive interpreter about his (her) expectational set, if not linguistically, then tacitly or gesturally, but with no less potency. Both the pre-arranged deontic background and the political interpretation of any meaningful utterance is *constantly being negotiated*, and not only between the sexes. In ordinary social relations a *subliminal civil war* actually rages. In this war, one deontic and political proposal after another tries to force its way to the surface, until either (a) everyone is exhausted by the effort and finds he (she) can live with some extension of the *status quo*, and, by simply withdrawing attention from the content, allows it to stand or (b) someone manages to formulate a new deontology, a social or a scientific revolution, which explicitly sets a new benchmark for worldly conversation and for the general level of cultural discourse. This is the normal *mechanism of collective intentionality*, and it is universally in play in history, in politics and in all manner of social life. Thus,

> NLSoc1.0: The subliminal civil war (the mechanism of degenerate collective intentionality).

In pure conversation however, this subliminal situation is completely reversed. Pure conversation requires everyone to assess *all* of the logical, political and deontic entailments of each meaningful proposition before the next one can be made. In pure conversation, there is no struggle of each against all to determine the meaning or significance of what was just said. Rather, each meaningful proposition is allowed a full and autonomous exhibition, and the deontic acceptance of its entailments is explicit, universal and subject to the respect of the free and equal players. The respect or dignity accorded to the pure conversational act is, at a minimum, a consequence of physics. In pure conversation, what is in play is the *impulse to experience meaning with exactitude*. When two or more gather for the sake of this impulse, the wave forms intrinsic to the individualities present unite and combine in a completely original way, and all find themselves in the presence of cosmic law and cosmic intelligence. Under these conditions, a pure, genuine and cosmic sublimity is both willed and experienced.

Now there is one thing to add to our account of meaning. Although the structure of meaning can be analyzed materially in terms of deontic background and political entailment, and under conditions of pure conversation perhaps in terms of wave mechanics, it needs to be recognized as well that meaning is irreducibly magical. If a sign, sound or mark *in itself* is said to have conditions of satisfaction, as it surely does when I signal the advance of the enemy by raising my arm, we are giving some ground to *magical thinking*. If meaning is the imposition of conditions of satisfaction on otherwise lifeless objects such as sounds, marks or even gestures, then something non-living can be said actually to have conditions that satisfy it. It is being said to have appetites and aversions. I see nothing wrong with entertaining this line of reasoning, and a similar one is used in the new field of *artificial life*. The sounds and marks that mean something are alive. The more acute, clear and rich those meanings are, the more alive they become. On this magical view, it is man's cosmic destiny to breathe life, Godlike, into material nature. We can do this by means of a social life that controls ordinary communication at the level of *meaning impulses*, the capacity to initiate a concept and to authorize it in a social body. Because magic has a structure, and because that structure is the structure of meaning, man will magicalize (spiritualize) the earth by controlling meanings in conversation. Thus,

HypPsy3.0: The theory of magic and the structure of magic.

Of course, one would not wish to be too liberal with the magical license, lest some truly irresponsible impulses be unleashed and legitimized. But if cosmic evolution does essentially involve the human being, and if the essence of cosmic intelligence is inside the human intelligence, then one begins to see what is necessary for a consensual understanding on this topic to develop. On Rudolf Steiner's anthroposophical picture, the angels live, move and have their being in the moral thoughts of the human being. Their ontology and their dimensionality begin on a level that very few of us have much, if any control over at all, the level of the *thought impulse*. Beyond them live the archangels, who organize cultural and racial genius and the great historical epochs. And so on, up a grand staircase into increasingly exalted domains and purposes. And of course, these domains and purposes determine individual experience after death and the disposition one brings into the next life. If these are realities, then conversation theory appears the best way to re-open the magical box, which has been with us since the Neolithic and has only recently been closed by modern materialism, and to produce for humanity an initiation science at once socially responsible and scientifically testable.

Chapter 8

LOVE

The one who came from farthest to my lodge, through deepest snows and most dismal tempests, was a poet. A farmer, a hunter, a soldier, a reporter, even a philosopher, may be daunted; but nothing can deter a poet, for he is actuated by pure love.
—THOREAU, *Walden*

LOVE MAKES THE WORLD GO AROUND. It is probably the fundamental cosmic law. It certainly would appear to be the fundamental law of social and mental activity, and perhaps even of life itself. Love represents, if anything does, the whole of the human potential.

Love is not well understood in material terms, nor are its energies in general well regulated or controlled. For something that contains the whole of the human future, it is probably time to start to learn how to engineer it socially. Some spiritual adepts claim to be able to reverse the discharge of the orgasm, and to direct it into the brain. The orgasmic reversal is probably the thing to understand if we are to learn to engineer the energies of love. The orgasm, which is still an unexplained physiological mystery, is far and away the best candidate for explaining love in cosmo-mechanical terms.

Pure conversation is a literal and ongoing orgasm, albeit in a supersensible world. Like the sexual discharge, its purpose is reproduction. Unlike the energy of the sex organs, however, its energies are articulate, fully conscious, and regenerative, and are directed (upward and backward) toward *ideal mental contents* along the spinal column and brain. The alternative direction, downward and outward into the blood and organs of the body, with its focus on material sensation, is merely animal and degenerative. Because of this *intellectual condition*, love taking place in conversation has more rarified and complex features than love between bedsheets. It is also considerably more dignified, calling out the best in human nature, which in essence is actually conservative, noble and morally responsible, and neither eliminative, beggarly nor compulsive. Let us say:

> CCMn2.0: Principle of ideal mental contents (intellectual condition).

The Social Duty Cluster

The basic conversational algorithm (CC23.1) represents the essential logic of love. There are several reasons to think this is true. One reason is the centrality to the algorithm of reproduction and reproducibility. *Reproduction* requires full and accurate attention given to the spirit of what was just expressed. Attention of this kind shines a light into the soul of the person being reproduced. This light produces a benign and total *self-consciousness*, which is essential to love. *Reproducibility* in its turn requires a careful attention to oneself as performer, who lives for the experience of the other. Focus in the experience of the other personality is also essential to love, because love is, above all, the expression of *selflessness*. Paradoxes aside, let us say:

> CCMn1.1: Principle of reproduction;
> CCMn1.2: Principle of reproducibility;
> CCSR1.3: Principle of self-consciousness;
> CCSP1.0: Principle of selflessness.

Another, more complicated reason to think the basic algorithm should be seen as the essence of love has to do with the overall function of conversation. Real conversation is about turning men and women into literal spirits. Some men (and some women) are less disposed than others, despite their attestations to the contrary, to function in the way required to meet that end. The algorithm is about helping these individuals transcend their dispositional handicaps.

Implicit in the basic algorithm is something called the Fundamental Duty Cluster, which derives from a conjunction of the principle of continuity (CCSIn1.0) and the principle of freedom (CCFr1.0). The principle of continuity says that pure conversation must involve a logical and energetically harmonious progression over time. Any action by any speaker in a conversation is the sounding of a kind of note, a sono-mechanical claim on the space that everyone is sharing.

If the conversation were a jazz performance, a suggestive key change by one of the performers would compel the rest of the ensemble to shift modality and adopt the new key. If the conversation were a classical music rehearsal, a wrong note would require the conductor to stop and address the problem. If the wrong note occurred during a public performance, anyone hearing it would have to wince, and possibly walk out, because a wrong note in a classical recital is a deontic violation. The situation is similar in pure conversation.

It must be remembered that freedom is the law of all expressions in conversation. In conversation, everyone is free to say whatever he (she) wants (principle of freedom, CCFr1.0), and the essence of freedom is universal assertability or universal acceptability (cf. NLM, CCTr1.0). Now, *suppose a speaker decides to invoke CCFr1.0, but speaks nonsense.* Suppose he says, for example,

(1) GATUUC. CATTUGATAATAUC.

Assume there is at least one person present who doesn't care to discuss nonsense, and *invokes the following rule*:

> CCLog1.7: Principle of reasonableness (no conversation is about nonsense).

In this case, because of a conflict of principles, a social duty arises, the *duty of the meta-conversation.* The conflict must be adjudicated in real time before the conversation can continue.

Now the original speaker must justify his (her) presumably free action. The alternative, that the hearer who objected to the speaker's utterance must justify his assertion of nonsense is ruled out by hypothesis – here, the speaker actually does utter nonsense. In this case, the speaker cannot appeal to reasonableness (CCLog1.7), but only to freedom (CCFr1.0). But the appeal to freedom under these conditions can now only be a violation of the following principle:

CCLog1.8: Principle of good faith (no conversation is grounded on bad faith).

The speaker after all has by definition accepted $CC_M SC$, the principle of the social contract. Basically, *the scales are tipped against the speaker*, three principles to one. The speaker's action must therefore have been compelled by a *pathological motivation*.

Notice what is occurring here. A *conflict of principles* invokes a meta-conversation, and a social duty. Under a conflict of principles, one of which will infallibly involve the principle of freedom (CCFr1.0), it is underdetermined which principle has priority, and some hashing out is necessary. Principles of proper conduct must be summoned and enumerated. A *violation of principle*, on the other hand, is readily adjudicated as pathology. No principle of conversation can be violated without implying pathology, and in the event of real social conflict, the rules which govern conversation should be rich enough to allow for the eventual determination of some actual violation. Actual conversations, after all and by and large, do tend to sustain themselves at some level in the face of conflict. Let us therefore say:

CCSp2.0: Principle of social pathology;
CCSp3.0: Principle of contractual enumeration (principle of hashing out).

So in the case of an actual pathology, a basic decision has to be made by the social organism. A person choosing to speak or compelled to speak irrationally forces its hand. It must respond to the irritation (the pathology) in the way that a body responds to disease. It must restore energetic balance by giving an *adequate amount* and the *right kind* of attention to the individual. Either it must heal itself by that mechanism, or it must die.

The nature of the Social Duty Cluster (CCSP2.3) is as follows:

D1 The stream of the conversation has been altered by an irrational force (e.g. a nonsensical content has been expressed);

D2 The expression was not a free action because it lacked universal legitimacy (it was nonsensical to at least one person present, and appeared to violate one or several principles of conversation);
D3 There is a pathogenic agent at work in the social organism (someone's free consciousness is disturbed);
D4 The social organism must be healed (must be restored to its prior continuity);
D5 Attention of the right sort must be deployed in the direction of the pathogen.

Now this turn from the substance of the conversation (whatever it was) to the disturbance in the consciousness of some individual who happens to be present is not easily tolerated by many. Nevertheless, *intelligent tolerance* is the essence of love. As every mother knows, in love one simply gives one's energy and attention to something that by some sort of right demands it, regardless of one's inclinations to the contrary. One simply does not know now what hope there is for what was developed conversationally up to that point. The conversation is now about the person disturbing the conversation, and that person has a basic right to the attention of all others. Call these,

CCSP2.1: The principle of tolerance;
CCSP2.2: The right of the anti-social.

Such a right, I think, is nothing more and nothing less than the right we each have to stand in the Presence of God and to hold conversation with Him. Here on earth, however, a stepped-down version of that birthright can be arranged, and that version is pure conversation. To submit oneself to universal judgment, to the living and intelligent regard of a group of focused individuals whose sole interest and intention is the continuity and circulation of energy in a universal living organism, is probably more or less what it will be like when one meets one's Maker in the afterlife. From time to time it will simply be necessary for everyone to stop and give energy and attention to someone who has momentarily lost the golden thread. To stop in this manner, to sacrifice everything gained up to that point, and to set things universally right with that individual is quite literally to be love.

Now, unless the person in Case 1 is clinically psychotic, in which case his (her) appearance in the conversation would be unlikely at the beginning, it remains inevitable that somehow the logic of his (her) position, and its genuine relevance to the conversation, can be discovered (c.f. $CC_M Rat3.2$, CCLog1.1). Much in the way of the brilliant demonstration by others may therefore need to be forgone, for the sake of reining in the wayward sheep, but ultimately, the entire conversation can be completed from his (her) point of view. In love, the meek inherit. Thus,

CCSIn7.0: The principle of sacrifice.

Now the foregoing is how things play out if everyone wants more than anything to keep the conversation alive. The alternative (Case 2) of course is to allow the conversation to die. On that alternative, the speaker never acknowledges that he (she) has spoken nonsense, thereby insisting that his (her) freedom is the paramount value. Under these conditions, conversation simply is not possible. Let us say:

CCEng1.1: The limiting condition (if it is not possible to actualize a universal judgment with respect to some current content, conversation is not possible).

The sacrifice of the conversation itself can still be a positive event. The situation is analogous to Christ's choice before Pilate. How could the Divine Being, by invoking his magical powers, quietly wriggle free of his terrible fate? He was forced by the circumstances he freely created to act out his Passion. Similarly, if there is no real capacity for conversation present, it is best formally to acknowledge the fact, if possible, and to act with dignity and blessing in its demise. Spiritually, principled sacrifice is the strongest possible social action to take, and it necessarily has causal world consequences, even if these are difficult to assess in the moment. Let us say:

CCSIn7.1: The principle of total sacrifice (sacrifice of the conversation);

CCSP2.3: The Social Duty Cluster.

The Principle of Sober Love

In pure conversation, all of the social mechanisms of ordinary love (attraction, admiration, adoration etc.) are at work, and other controlling mechanisms are added. A person who may have triggered one's sexual interest, and who may have responded subtly with "feelers" of his (her) own, is now required to function in an enhanced social situation. In this situation, he (she) is subject to the judgment of all others, not just to the peculiar judgments of a possible lover. Whereas heretofore he (she) appeared under the form of an ideal projection (a content of individual attraction) for one or more people present, he (she) is now required to function under his (her) own *actual content* in a way that satisfies everyone present.

Here the result may be fortunate (the person may prove to be quite competent and even manifestly like a god), in which case the person suddenly transcends the limitations projected on him (her) by his (her) would be lover (lovers). In this case, he (she) appears less as an object of infatuation and more as an object of legitimate respect, if not awe. Alternatively, the result may be less fortunate, in which case the object of love becomes an object of compassion. In either case, illusions are vanquished and love is raised to an objective mode. Everyone develops a certain respect for everyone else. A sober and realistic love sets the tone for this and future social situations, in which humans beings begin to resemble actual spirits. Let us say:

CCLov1.0: Principle of sober love (principle of realism in love).

The principle of sober love is good news for the beautiful and the not-so-beautiful alike. Physical beauty is generally taken unconsciously as a sign of personal and moral superiority, while the absence of beauty is generally interpreted unconsciously as a sign of moral depravity. This unjust cosmic condition on human experience is directly remediated by the principle of sober love. What matters under this highly social condition is that one's actual moral capacities be exhibited and subjected to universal judgment. Under these conditions, sooner or later, love simply issues forth. One finds oneself able and willing to love one's neighbor, and even one's enemy, regardless of how he (she) looks or sounds, simply because it is part of the physics of social nature to do so. In love, we sense the life body of the other person acutely, in intimate and reciprocal penetration with our own life. This divine modality is indifferent to outward appearances and even to personalities. It is produced by a universal moral intuition of how things actually are in the supersensible worlds, and in this intuition we sense that its power and its bliss go on and on endlessly, through the geometries of mystical appearances and objects, and out into the cosmic spaces.

Needless to say, a situation in which these noumenal cosmic intuitions of lovers, gods and crystalline perfect forms permeate and penetrate not only consciousness, but objective nature herself, is a great and grand scenario, and one we cannot expect to produce in real time without considerable work and effort. However, I believe it is a universal desire in humanity, probably the universal desire, to accomplish and to participate in just this result. For this reason, it is not only the possibility of the City of God touching down on and coming to rest in Earth existence, but the necessity of that eventual outcome that any theory of conversation must account for. Conversations, all of them, from the most sublime to the most ridiculous, are about the Divine Intuition. All conversation is searching, with an acute and ideal will, for the love that underlies it and gives it substance. Let us say:

CCDiv1.1: Principle of the City of God (principle of divine cosmic evolution).

Love enters conversation in another way as well, through the requirement that all conversational actions are actions one loves to take. If a conversational action is loved, it will not be mistaken. It will satisfy the cosmo-mechanical intentionality of all perceptions. But the love must be authentic. If it is somehow insincere, the art will fail. This requirement, the love of the conversational deed, is suggested by several of the conversational principles already discussed: the principle of sincerity (CCTr1.1), the principle of art (CCArtSC1.0), the principle of inspiration (CCSIn3.1), the principle of fundamental ontology (CCUniRep4.0). But in essence, the principle is one of *motivation*. All real conversation is motivated by love. Let us say:

> CCUniRep4.3: Principle of motivation by love (love of the deed).

How and why individuals will infallibly find themselves rightly motivated for conversation has to do with the intrinsic beauty and sublimity of real conversation. A living art simply has this motivating effect on the human being. The human being loves conversational art because conversational art is an exercise of love. Only the lover is lovable, and, for the human being, conversation is the great lover. Therefore, the human being in real conversation loves. This motivational outcome is as inevitable and as necessary a worldly principle as water flowing downhill or warmth quickening the buds and flowers of spring. Let us say:

> NLPsy9.0: Law of love.

Competition, the great principle of earthly life, is in conversation transfigured by the many actions of love. To be sure, even in pure conversation, beings remain in a war of each against all, but the idea of this war is neither brute survival nor economic freedom (wealth). It is rather a war of cultural ascendancy, a competition to determine what values in life as a whole are paramount and which are less important. Those which are used and which enter the mainstream of human culture, such as Judeo-Christian moral ideas, are victorious in the competition. Those which fall into disuse and remain outside the mainstream, such as the communistic ideas of Lenin and Mao, are vanquished. But with the advent of rigorous conversation practices, those values and cultural ideas made subject to competition and survival will be not so much abstract intellectual contents as subtle *spiritual events*. Under the influence of conversation theory and practice, human culture will become a literal competition among the principals (the spirits) of the cosmos itself. In love, and only in love, can the full scope and extent of these cosmic battles be witnessed and even entered upon. Let us say:

> CCDiv1.2: Principle of cosmic competition (principle of culture and counter-culture).

The Threefold Social Order

Notwithstanding the wide-open nature of cultural selection as it must be practiced under conditions of pure conversation, I feel it is important at the outset to introduce a certain bias into the debate. The chief practical problem in seeing how pure conversation could become a viable institution in contemporary or future social life is the cultural pressure placed on individual thought and action by the market system of economic life. Under the market system, the human being is obligated to enter a life of prostitution. People in general are under such tremendous financial pressure to maintain and improve their standard of living (at the expense of a well-formed astral body) that it becomes almost impossible to imagine them putting serious energy and attention into activity that attempts to harness the cosmic energy of pure love. One should be under no illusions that astral love is a very demanding master.

The American economist and philosopher Henry George (1839–1897) showed that it is not market economics *per se* that leads to the diminishment and poverty of human spiritual life, whose true instinct and destiny is infinite love and infinite bliss among the spaces of the cosmos. Rather, it is a misapplication of market principles to a single factor that is neither in itself a commodity nor something that should, by right, be treated as a commodity. That factor is land, and to seize, to buy or to sell land as if it were something that could be made by human industry leads to fundamental distortions of human nature and human society.

No one who needs to think about paying a rent that, by economic law, takes away every bit of surplus he (she) is able by honest labor to produce can be seriously bothered with the demanding work of fundamental ontology and love. But Henry George showed that this appropriation by the landlord of labor's surplus, and the inequities and consequent vulgarization of culture as a whole, is not a necessary economic condition on human life. It is only a historical extension of the politics of conquest, enslavement and social stratification that has marked human societies from their beginnings. But to repeat, arbitrary power relations are not economically necessary. In fact, our economies would produce much more wealth if it were not possible to invest capital in land.

Be that as it may, it is also true that no very great obstacle, economic or otherwise, exists to taking the first small steps toward a culture of enlightened spirits on earth. In our day and age, the culture of conversation is a political, not an economic project. What is important now is to get the logic of pure conversation right, to determine the true form of the social contract and to subscribe that contract in a modest way. Once that is accomplished, and a few talented practitioners are up and running, larger social questions, such as economic disparities and educational objectives broadly speaking can be discussed. Let us distinguish, in setting the framework for a culture of cosmic love:

NLSoc2.0: The cultural life;
NLSoc3.0: The economic life;
NLSoc4.0: The life of rights.

The Etheric Child

Finally, any discussion of love cannot be completed without some indications in the direction of the *etheric child*. This is the entity or function that Rudolf Steiner foresaw would be the principle of all natural and sexual selection in the distant human future. In this future, Steiner said, human consciousness, human experience and in a sense even human existence would spring not from the material action of the sexes and from the competitive battle for physical and economic survival, but from the action of speech and of thought itself. In short, the humans of the future will spring directly from the action of love. Pure conversation, as I have defined it here, is consistent with that picture. The aim and objective of pure conversation is to create something living out of the spaces between and among human beings. The aim and objective of pure conversation is to reverse and harness the cosmic potential of the orgasm.

That "something living" to be created by pure conversation is the content (the *logos*) of what can be made a matter of universal and reciprocal contact in a formal and extended social situation. It is an etheric entity, autonomous, profound, often fantastic, in the manner of a deep spiritual dream. It is, in fact, made precisely of the stuff of dreams, whatever that is. It is the body of a living social organism. Under the conditions I am describing here, it is quite literally a love child, a form produced out of the mutual and ecstatic wills of individuals working together in a highly social circumstance. The difference between this child and its biological counterpart is that this child is produced in etheric space under conditions of perfect responsibility, self-consciousness and moral will. This child is an ideal form appearing, mystically, in real time. Let us say:

> CCLov2.0: Principle of the etheric child (the reversal of the orgasm).

Perhaps we can most perfectly account for love and its progressive manifestations in human experience by appealing once again to Plato's Socrates. When we are in love with someone, he says, there are clearly the elements of physical and emotional need and fulfillment. But the lover is never merely carnal and merely romantic. The lover is ideal. He (she) is *ultimately good*. We never behold the flaws in the beloved as evil. Evil is not an essential part of human nature, but only an occlusion of the good. What is apparently beheld in the lover is something that is good in ourselves, and a mature understanding recognizes that this good is our own self-knowledge and our own self-mastery. In short, this good is our own spiritual completion.

This then, Aristophanes, is the right way of approaching and of being initiated into the mysteries of love. Begin with examples of beauty in this world, including examples of physical beauty, and use them as steps to ascend continually to that absolute beauty, to that essence of beauty in one's own mind. (*Symposium*)

Chapter 9

INSTITUTIONS

They had journeyed thus far by the west-ways, for they had much to speak of with Elrond and with Gandalf, and here they lingered still in converse with their friends. Often long after the hobbits were wrapped in sleep they would sit together under the stars, recalling the ages that were gone and all their joys and labours in the world, or holding council, concerning the days to come. If any wanderer had chanced to pass, little would he have seen or heard, and it would have seemed to him only that he saw grey figures, carved in stone, memorials of forgotten things now lost in unpeopled lands. For they did not move or speak with mouth, looking from mind to mind; and only their shining eyes stirred and kindled as their thoughts went to and fro.

—J. R. R. TOLKEIN, *The Return of the King*

INSTITUTIONAL REALITY, FAMILIAR to and intimately utilized by the denizens of all human society is, I think, the actual nature of human consciousness and human experience. Both human institutions, which are things like contracts, constitutions and the common law, and human consciousness, by which we basically mean experience in the human mode, are what they are *because everyone thinks they are what they are*. In the case of social institutions, that claim is not controversial – a dollar bill is money because everyone accepts it as money; a state or federal official is what he (she) is because everyone thinks he (she) has that status.

In the case of consciousness or experience on the other hand, the claim may seem quite unlikely. There is, or appears to be, after all, a material world that is not only independent of what everyone may happen to think, but that of itself actually forces everyone to think in certain ways. Clearly we all walk around upright on the surface of a rather large cosmic body, and some pretty forced reasoning would be required to convince most of us that our experience of that fact depends on the structure of what we are thinking, and not on what conditions on the surface of our planet actually do to us.

Yet there are reasons to think the former interpretation may be at least partially correct. In itself, what is "the surface of the earth?" Is it not clear that in itself and outside of time, the earth is really some unimaginable vortex in cosmic space? Is it not clear that our own motions within this vortex, if such motions there really be, are in reality even more unimaginable, to the point where it is reasonable to suppose that we ourselves stretch out through cosmic space in an etheric reality that may or may not bear the familiar relation to "the surface of the earth?" Is it not reasonable to think that the unimaginableness of our actual and transcendental cosmic condition is made manageable by certain mental presuppositions, categories or schemata that we bring to our situation as *filters*, that allow only experience of our type to take place in us, even though our true situation may justify experience of quite another kind?

Kant certainly thought something like this line of deduction was valid, and tried to show how experience (human consciousness) was made possible by something called *reason*. I want to suggest that reason is nothing more (and nothing less) than a cosmic form of institutional reality. Reason (language, logic) is a mental filter on the world itself that not only makes our species of experience possible, but that is legislated and administered by a bureaucracy of etheric and astral entities, of which we in reality are one such, that extends seamlessly back, out or through the cosmos to a primal dimension and intensity that we, in the poverty of our capacity for seeing things as they are in reality, can only call "God." Let us then say:

> NLPsy10.0: Law of institutional reality (law of the mental filter).

The scientific materialist will likely find an ontological move like the above unjustifiably complicated and arbitrary, and probably not

needed to explain or control consciousness and experience, in view
of our current and expanding knowledge of neuroscience and psy-
chopharmacology, to take two salient examples. But scientific materialism is actually quite helpless to explain human freedom and
to control human conversation, much less to give these a form that
is ontologically satisfying to the natural values and spiritual aspira-
tions of the individual. Scientific materialism can and will never give
rigorous conversation a truly human dimension. To do these things,
it will be necessary to produce not only an institutional theory (and
an institutional reality) that controls and intensifies conversation, but
also a single consensual and ontologically satisfying knowledge of
spiritual realities and spiritual facts. For a truly accurate social science, one which extends to the core of human consciousness and
human experience, no other aim, object or protocol will do.

Now, to outline the basic theory of institutions, we define:

    (1) Institutional reality (x) $\leftrightarrow$ Everyone thinks (institutional
       reality (x)).

Already we can see how institutions rest mysteriously on thoughts
alone. They are undeniably realities, but they are realities that float
above the world of nature and natural law. They are already transcendental entities, and as such are one step closer than most material
objects are to the supersensible worlds of dreams, spirit vision and
the ideal Platonic forms. However likely or unlikely the particular
exemplification, from the Catholic eucharist to recess at a maximum
security Federal penitentiary, institutional experience is spiritual experience.

Now the foregoing definition admits of some further analysis. Institutions are organized on the basis of *status functions*. All institutions,
from the most pompous and grandiloquent, such as the coronation of
a British monarch, to the most ordinary and commonplace, such as
the naming of a newborn baby, are essentially the confirmation of
a status on some material token or entity. That entity may suggest
the status or function by its intrinsic form, as when an appropriately
shaped and weighted bone becomes a "weapon," or the function may

be imposed arbitrarily, as when a coin of a certain shape, weight and embossing becomes a "dollar." But in either or any case, an institution is a concept, a rule or a function that returns a bivalent satisfaction value. If X counts as Y in some context, C, then Y is an institution, and we say the function "counts as" is satisfied. If X does not count, then Y is not an institution, or at least not the institution that was imagined, and "counts as" is not satisfied. Thus:

$$(2)\ Y = F_C(X)$$

where F is the status function "counts as," X is some physical token, such as a dollar bill, Y is the assignment or institution, in this case US currency, and C is the universe of minds (the context) what makes the whole thing real.

All words and all sentences, therefore, and even all gestures and subliminal signs in conversation partake of this basic structure. The acoustic blast coming from the larynx, the turn of the head, the unbroken stare may in themselves be quite insignificant and uninterpretable, but in a conversational context each of these is transformed by a status function operating in the mind of each participant into a concept or a meaning that has a binding effect on the cosmic reality of the situation. Because of the satisfaction of the status function (because something is counted as something else in the current context), a human (an institutional) reality is created. That acoustic blast meant, "I request (x)" or "I declare (y);" that turn of the head meant "I assert (v)" or "I express (w);" that stare meant, "I promise (z)."

A satisfaction value should be viewed as a *self-sense*. Whether some physical token counts or does not count as a concept (an institution) under certain conditions not only makes it possible to experience that token (to be conscious of that token), but it makes it possible for the agent to experience (to be conscious of) himself (herself) *as a self*. This process of finding oneself satisfied by and thereby recognizing objects, situations and events in the world is so seamless, pervasive and ongoing that it takes special and extraordinary efforts of will and imagination to find oneself in the presence of things and events that transpire on an order of magnitude beyond it. But these limits of the self nature are precisely what pure conversation seeks to transcend. Pure conversation is about locating, stabilizing and controlling institutions (concepts) that exist outside the limits of mere material selfhood, in the starry territories governed by angels and other cosmic entities, whose society and whose purposes transcend and yet involve our own, quite literally in the structure of our thoughts, in ways we have not learned to imagine, to intuit or to articulate.

This transcendence of the self-nature may be somewhat more congenial with the anti-representational view of consciousness and experience (see page 118) than with the foregoing analysis, which is materialist and representational. On the anti-representational view, the contents and structure of our moral and social impulses lie outside our self-sense from the beginning. They are not complicated, at least in paradigmatic cases, by any egotism or self-consciousness. On this view in fact, the self-sense is a cosmic illusion. On the anti-representational view, what is going on inside us as inner experience apparently bound together by an ego or a self is in reality a set of probability functions which just happen to cohere because of the physical conditions (temperature, pressure, volume, etc.) under which our body is able to function. On this view, institutional reality is just a set of gambles that happen to pay off consistently, and is no more transcendental than the world of nature, which is likewise a set of gambles.

Nevertheless, pure conversation seeks to alter certain of these conditions materially, whatever their ontological status, for the purpose of giving rise to a new set of probability functions, or institutional features, whichever you prefer. The physical condition I think we need to pay attention to here is blood flow, and in general fluid dynamics in the human body. Although blood flow in general is hardly something we would want to call "institutional" or "conceptual," it may be possible to show that certain types of blood flow in human beings are quite relevant to conscious and sub-conscious representations. Acute self-consciousness and embarrassment do generally correspond with specific movements of the blood, and the principle may be a general one with all moments of spiritual intelligence, which are likewise self-conscious, although in a positive sense.

Still, blood flow can only be a correlate of the reality that is brought into being by thinking about it in a categorical fashion. The actual reality here, whether it is represented somehow and placed under the control of the ego, or whether it is merely caused by finely tuned natural conditions, is a subtle field phenomenon of undetermined composition. But finding a physical correlate to a spiritual mechanism would be a clear scientific advance. And if this is the correct correlate, things may work reasonably from the bottom up as well – if we could somehow induce exactly the right blood flow in the individual, we may be able inductively to produce something that can pass for spiritual experience. Let us say:

HypPsy9.0: Hypothesis on the blood;
HypPsy9.1: Blood circulation is specifically restricted by spiritual contents.

Technological spirituality, however, is hardly the objective of pure conversation. Quite the opposite. Pure conversation, which relies on the God-given and naturally selected faculties of will, imagination, ordinary language and moral intuition is a natural spirituality. Its politics are the politics of the ancient spirits, and centuries and centuries of human karma. The new humanity, by way of contrast, which is all but certain to arise from the joining of bodies, genes and brains to molecular machines, exogenous implants and vast computing power, will have its own cold and seductive politics and values. The two streams of humanity are bound to diverge culturally, and even biologically. Whether a mutual accommodation can be reached between the two races, call them the naturals and the cyborgs, or whether one stream will dominate and enslave the other remains to be seen. Given the tremendous economic and political power that are certain to accrue to the cyborgs, ascent into the etheric worlds may prove to be, for the naturals, a survival mechanism as much as anything else.

Be that as it may, it seems all but certain that the representational/anti-representational debate will keep the pure conversationists wondering about themselves for a long time. The solution to the dilemma may be to view the natural human being in two modes—the egoic and the not-egoic. The former is he (she) whom we encounter when *judgments* are the appropriate modality, when we are trying to control things either inside ourselves or in our environment. These are the modes of the military general, of the magician, of the corporate executive. Under these conditions, it does indeed seem accurate to suppose that we represent to or in ourselves the conditions that satisfy our current state (status) of intending. But when we are at our best and most lovable, when we are purely social beings, we simply *express* our inner condition, as when we surrender ourselves to our lover, or to sleep, or to God. Under these conditions, and these are the epitome of pure conversation, we are more like waves in the cosmic ether, autonomous but indifferent to care and obligation, like the images in the dream of some great cosmic intelligence.

This latter may be more than a metaphor. It may be our true cosmic condition. In reality, if the possibility can be entertained, the institution of pure conversation is quite a bit more pervasive and instrumental in this world than it may appear. The angels and cosmic hierarchies function in precisely the way I am outlining in this essay. Among them, thought and intuition are material actions. Among them, events and contents concatenate out of an inner necessity, and give rise to etheric realities that obey their own intrinsic laws. We ourselves are among these realities. Our actual self-conscious thoughts and contents, the spiritual images in our dreams, and even the health and vitality of our blood and of our body are the outcomes of conversation between and among the hierarchies of spirits that pervade the cosmos in its supersensible dimensions. We are actually the product of a great cosmic conversation that extends up and back through the sensible and the supersensible dimensions and through the functional hierarchies of spirits all the way to God. That at least is a coherent picture of our condition, and it certainly makes more sense than materialism. Let us say:

HypPhy3.0: The theory of the cosmic origins.

From the foregoing it should be clear why the theory of institutions is of paramount importance in conversation theory. Pure conversation is <u>the</u> human institution that cries out for legitimate foundations. Once that foundation is achieved, the world will begin to sparkle from the inside like a luminous jewel. All manner of degeneracy, vulgarity and corruption will either be eliminated through disuse or will be partitioned away by free choice. Assuming the conflict of cultures is settled satisfactorily, and in favor of a general Judeo-Christian morality (i.e. in favor of universal individualism), a culture of art, spiritual reality and inner human beauty will prevail on earth, and the impulses of materialism will decline in strength. A new City will rise up out of the ideals of the human spirit, and Man will govern Himself as a rank of Angels in the spiritual cosmos. All of this will be made possible, and can only be made possible, by an accurate, sensitive and thorough incorporation and utilization by society of the transcendental (spiritual) nature of human institutions.

The status function "counts as" in its many and various appearances in human society and human experience has an equivalent form expressed in terms of institutional power. The form is:

(3) Everybody accepts (S has power (S does A))

where S is an agent or functional entity and A is an action or function performed by that agent or entity. Thus, for dollar bills:

(4) Everybody accepts (the dollar bill has power (the dollar bill purchases or can purchase one dollar's worth of economic value).

Now the situation is identical with the words and sentences (the contents) in conversation. In cases where the meaning of the current content is unambiguous and interpreted identically, as it must be in pure conversation, everybody accepts that that content has the power to do whatever it does to the *context* of the conversation:

(5) $C' = C \cap p$

where C is the current context, p is the current proposition and C' is the updated context. One can see here how power in conversation is a power of sorting or selecting – disused references are abandoned and new references are introduced. The analogies with biological (evolutionary) selection are apparent.

An institution that allows words and sentences to move autonomously, on their own trajectories, as though they were actual agents with their own minds and laws, is a necessary condition on spiritualizing conversation. Conversational content under rigorous and formal conditions is really Inspiration from a supersensible world, a domain of spiritual causes with material consequences. Such Inspiration is the essence of consciousness in the human individual, and above and beyond all chemistry, physiology and postural alignment, it is an institutionally generated and institutionally administered impulse descending from the Prime Cause of all things, sensible and supersensible. It is the social action of the gods, the politics of spirits and the etheric power of material manifestation out of spiritual causes. It is the intervention of the sacred in the inertia of the profane. That at any rate is the theory. Let us say:

CCSR1.2: Principle of autonomy in conversational content.

Appendix A

THE ART OF
GOETHEAN CONVERSATION

CONVERSING, AS GOETHE conceived it, is the art of arts. The very place in his works where the subject finds mention lets us glimpse its singular rank in his esteem. This is the key scene of his fairy tale, "The Green Snake and the Beautiful Lily." There, the four kings enthroned in the subterranean mystery temple are roused to the dawning of a New Age of Man when the serpent, made luminous by the gold she has swallowed, penetrates with light into their dark sanctuary. The following dialog takes place:

> "Whence came you hither?" asked the golden king.
> "Out of the clefts where the gold dwells," replied the serpent.
> "What is more glorious than gold?"
> "Light."
> "What is more quickening than light?"
> "Conversation."

Unless one understands what Goethe meant, one can feel disappointed at the serpent's answer, which scarcely seems the revelation one expected. For is conversation as we know it in the Twentieth Century really more glorious than gold, more quickening than light? Hardly! We attach the term to every casual exchange, to the most idle, inconsequential chitchat. Surely, we feel, the term must have come down in the world since Goethe's day, suffering the severest diminution in its slide.

That this is indeed the case becomes apparent when we recall the salons of earlier centuries where great minds came together for significant talk. These occasions were of a wholly different order from our social happenings. They were disciplined, where ours are chaotic.

They were built around a common purpose, mutually enriching rather than depleting. It is impossible to picture the participants in a salon all talking at once, babbling away on as many subjects as there were pairs of conversationalists present. No! Rather, the star of a theme hung over the assemblage as over a pool studded with crystals, and the responsively scintillating crystal intellects took turns voicing the reflections awakened in them.

Goethean conversations differ at least as much again from those of the salon as did the salon from today's cocktail party. Their purpose is to call forth a fullness of spiritual life, not to stage displays of intellectual fireworks. They have nothing in common with the salon's formal play of light points sparkling in cold starlit glitter. Instead, they strive to enter the sunward realm of living thoughts where a thinker uses all of himself as a tool of knowledge, where, in the manner of his thinking, he takes part as a creative spirit in the ongoing process of the cosmos.

This is to say that a true Goethean conversation takes place across the threshold, in the etheric world, where thoughts are intuitions that break through into the realm of First Cause.

Lesser types of interchange never do this: they remain mere mentalizing, speculation, argument, a recounting of experience, an offering of opinion, a reporting. At their worst, a mindless associative rambling.

While most of these lesser forms of exchange can be made to serve useful purposes, the fact that they remain on this side of the threshold condemns them to spiritual barrenness. They leave Earth and those who take part in them unfulfilled. They cannot overcome the isolation with which every man born since Adam feels afflicted.

True conversations have another power. As the participants strive to enter the world of living thoughts together, each attunes his intuitive perception to the theme. He does so in the special atmosphere engendered by approaching the threshold of the spiritual world, a mood of supernatural attentive listening, of the most receptive openness to the life of thought into which he and his companions are now entering.

In such an attitude the consciousness of all who share it shapes itself into a single chalice to contain that life. Partaking of that divine nutriment they partake also of communion, of fellowship. They live the Grail experience of modern man.

We have found Goethe depicting conversation as the art of arts. If it is indeed such, and we aspire to it, what does its practice require of us? Surely no amount of inspired groping will suffice. Techniques of a very special order must be cultivated.

Perhaps the first prerequisite is to be aware that the spiritual world beyond the threshold wishes every bit as keenly to be known to us as we wish to know it. It does not have to be taken by assault. Rather, it comes gladly to meet us, much as a wise and loving teacher responds to the warmth of a student's interest. No one genuinely eager to approach such a teacher with the proper reverence fails to elicit his responses. The spiritual world is no less eager to meet our interest. We recall Christ's assurance of this, "Seek and you shall find. Knock and it shall be opened unto you."

The seeker's attitude thus proves a magically evoking wand that, like the rod of Moses, unlocks the flow of spiritual life. One must know this to be a fact, both in one's own and in others' cases. Then the group's consciousness becomes indeed a common vessel in which to receive such illumination as the world beyond the threshold may, on each given occasion, find it suitable to offer.

One cannot, however, step with a single stride from ordinary thought and chatter into Goethean conversation. The latter requires the most loving preparation. Thoughts must first be conceived like children, and then brooded out in the spirits of the thinkers. To this end, the theme of the meeting is set in advance. Each member of the group lives with it as a developing concern in his meditation. As the day of the foregathering draws near, he begins to anticipate the coming together of a festival of light which, if he and his fellows have done their work well, will lead to their illumination by the spiritual world.

What specifically is meant by "work" here?

Certainly not the production of any finished concepts, the amassing of quotations from authoritative sources, the getting up of a resume of reading done. Thinking and study engaged in prior to a meeting rather serve the purpose of rousing the soul to maximum activity so that it may come into the presence of the spirit all perception. Work of this sort is a warming up, a brightening of consciousness to render the soul a dwelling place hospitable to insight. One must be willing to sacrifice previous thinking, as one does in the second stage of meditation, in order to clear the scene for fresh illumination.

The principle here is the same as that advanced by Rudolf Steiner when he advised Waldorf teachers to prepare their lessons painstakingly, but then be ready to sacrifice the prepared plan at the dictate of circumstances which may point to an entirely fresh approach to their material. If one is well prepared, he said, one will find the inspiration needed. Indeed, the principle is common to all esoteric striving: invite the spirit by becoming spiritually active, and then hold yourself open to its visitation.

Those who come to the meeting place thus prepared will not bring the street in with them in the form of all sorts of distracting chatter. One does not, after all, approach the threshold in an ordinary mood, and where an approach is prepared, the scene in which the encounter takes place becomes a mystery temple atmosphere. Conventional courtesies to the person in the next chair, comments on the weather, the transacting of a bit of business are all completely out of tune and keeping.

To abstain from chatter means learning to live without any sense of discomfort in poised quiet. A very special regard for and tolerance of silence is, after all, a *sine qua non* of esoteric life. It is under this heading that conversations also belong. This means an about face from accustomed ways. In ordinary social intercourse, words must flow or there is no proof of relating; silence signals breakdowns in communication. However, as one grows in awareness of the threshold, words for words' sake come to seem disturbers of the peace. Unnecessary utterance intrudes upon and destroys the concentrated inner quiet that serves as a matrix for the unfolding life of intuition.

Conversations rest as much on being able to preserve silence as on speaking. When it comes to the latter, one can find no better guide to the ideal than is offered in another piece of Goethean insight. The poet saw *necessity* as art's criterion. "Here is necessity, here is art." One can sharpen one's sense of the necessary to the point where a conversation develops like a living organism, every part essential and in balance, each contributor taking pains to lift and hold himself above the level of unshaped outpourings. To achieve true conversations, one must, in short, build with the material of intuition. To reach this height, everything of a personal sentient nature must be sacrificed. Only then can the conversation find its way to necessity.

When it does so, it becomes a conversation with the spiritual world as well as with one's fellow earthlings. Though groups vary greatly, a good deal of practice is usually needed to grow into a capacity for Goethean converse. Most individuals today are so habituated to discussion that they can hardly conceive higher levels of exchange. We are conditioned to earth, but the etheric realm has become a stranger to us.

Several means exist to school oneself in etheric thinking. A prime one is, of course, meditation as Anthroposophy teaches it. Another is an ever repeated study of Rudolf Steiner's *Philosophy of Freedom*, carried on with special attention to the way this book, which starts out on the customary ground of philosophical-intellectual argument, suddenly deserts it to lift, winged, into realms where every thought quickens and is free, creative deed. Simply to follow that metamorphosis is to receive an infusion of etheric forces whereby one's own thinking is enlivened and one's mind it tuned to intuitive perception.

A like transformation is brought about by steeping oneself in fairy tales and great poetry. Rhythms and images teem with spiritual life, and as one absorbs them one can feel one's own life being magically quickened.

It is wholly contrary to a truly modern community building concept to lean on leaders in a conversation. Rather does the creation of a Grail Cup consciousness require an intact circle of fully active, responsible individuals whose only leader is the spiritual world. If, before coming together, every such individual brings the theme of the meeting alive in himself and then, arrived there, suppresses the thoughts he has had while offering the life they have engendered to the spirit, the spirit will not fail to bestow fresh insight on a gathering prepared to receive it. This can be experienced again and again. One has only to be active and keep the way clear, knowing that "where two or more are gathered in my name, there am I in the midst of you."

The hope of the Presence can be strengthened by learning to listen to one's fellowmen in exactly the way one would listen to the spiritual world: evocatively, with reverence, refraining from any trace of reaction, making one's own soul a seedbed for others' germinal ideas. This is not to imply that the listener surrenders the least measure of discrimination. He weighs what he hears. But he does so in a novel manner, cleansing himself of sympathy and antipathy in order to serve as an objective sounding board against which the words of the speaker ring true or false.

Thus the speaker is brought to hear himself and weigh his own utterances. Correction, in the sense of an awakening, is there without the others sitting in judgment on him. Nor is this all. Listening evocatively is a sunlike deed. It rays the warmth and light of interest into the thought life, quickening the circle and encouraging it to a veritable burgeoning.

A question often asked by those who become interested in exploring conversations is, "How does one go about choosing themes?" Certainly not in the arbitrary way this is usually done. One cannot, as perhaps happened in the salon, seek out the intellectually most appealing theme, nor as in today's discussion group, run one's finger down a list of Timely Topics trying to light on the most timely. Instead, burning questions that have been harbored in the souls of the participants will seek the light, questions that have sprung from a heart's concern with matters of the spirit and are therefore already full of life and fire and rooted in something deeper than the intellect. These will burst out of their own vitality to claim the attention of the meeting.

Often a theme teems with such fullness of life that it leads through a long series of metamorphoses requiring many meetings for its exploration. Themes of this kind are especially valuable, because they tend to become lifelong spiritual concerns of all the members, and it is easy to see how indissolubly conversations about such matters link the conversers.

For a conversation to become a work of art, its life must be given form within a framework. Otherwise, it would struggle on amorphously. The framework that keeps conversations shaped is built in part out of temporal elements, in part of a very simple ritual. These are the invariable rules of esoteric practice. It will be found desirable to fix the exact time of both beginning and ending meetings, and to keep punctually to it. Everyone who intends to be present understands that he should arrive well beforehand to prepare himself to help launch the evening's activity in a gathered mood.

The ritual consists of rising and speaking together a line or more chosen for its spiritually orienting content, for example, "Ex Deo nascimur, In Christo morimur, Per Spiritum Sanctum reviviscimus." (Of God we are born, in Christ we die, Through the Holy Spirit we live again.) The same of another meditation may be spoken at the end of the meeting, again exactly at a predetermined hour.

It may be feared that rigid time limits inhibit the free unfolding of the conversation. This fear proves ungrounded. A painter's inspiration is not limited by the size of his canvas. Rather do limits serve in every art form as awakeners, sharpening awareness of what can be accomplished, and composition always adapts itself intuitively to the given space.

To make a composition "all of one piece," as it must be if it is to rank as art, the conversing circle needs to take unusual measures to preserve unity. Here again, there is a vast difference between a discussion and a conversation. In the former, few feel the least compunction about engaging in asides. Disruptive and rude though these are, and betraying conceit in their implication that what one is muttering to one's neighbor is of course of far more interest that what the man who has the floor is saying, they are not as final a disaster as when they take place in a conversation. Discussions base themselves on intellect, and intellectual thinking tends naturally to separateness.

Conversations are an order of thought in which illumined hearts serve as organs of intelligence, and the tendency to hearts is to union. The conversation group must make itself into a magic circle. The least break in its Grail cup wholeness would let precious light substance generated by the meeting drain away. Sensitive participants will feel asides and interruptions to be nothing less than a cutting off of the meeting from the spiritual world.

Many individuals feel that no conversations could ever match the inspiration of a top flight lecture. Hence, they tend to think conversing is a waste of time much better spent reading lectures or listening to them. No doubt, lectures serve important functions. Painstakingly prepared, they convey concentrations of spiritual substance to listeners, who sit down as it were to a meal someone else has placed before them. But, extending the analogy, dyed-in-the-wool lecture goers do all their eating at restaurants, never learning the lovely art of homemaking.

There is something woefully one-sided in such a way of life. Not only does it avoid responsibility and neglect opportunities for creative growth; it remains childishly dependent in the most important phase of human evolution, when one should be progressing from having truth revealed to discovering truth by one's own activity. Rudolf Steiner was no friend of dependency in any form. He seldom told people the solution to a problem, and then only when exceptional pressures of time required it. This is what the times demand of us, that we become spiritually self-active, learning to draw sustenance from the spiritual world for Earth's renewal. Goethean conversations will be found an ideal schooling for this foremost task.

Marjorie Spock, 1983
East Sullivan, Maine

Appendix B

THE CONVERSATIONAL CONTRACT

META RULES

Rule on the Social Contract

$CC_M SC$: Only individuals who have explicitly accepted the rules generally believed to constitute pure conversations can participate in them (principle of the social contract).

Rules on Rationality

$CC_M Rat1.0$: All conversation has a logical (describable) structure.

$CC_M Rat2.0$: The background principles, rules and meta-rules generally believed to underlie pure conversation are each universal and constitutive, and will be recognized as such and utilized instinctively by any rational person (*a priority* principle).

$CC_M Rat3.0$: Principle of the meta-conversation (formality condition).

$CC_M Rat3.1$: Principle of testing.

$CC_M Rat3.2$: Principle of mutual interpretability.

$CC_M Rat4.0$: Principle of intuitive unity (principle of disambiguation).

$CC_M Rat5.0$: Principle of the index (principle of logical assignment and logical satisfaction).

$CC_M Rat5.1$: Principle of the self-conscious index (principle of *jnana yoga*).

Rule on Tolerance

$CC_M Tol$: Each background principle, rule and meta-rule underlying pure conversation confers rights but not strict duties on the individuals participating in the conversation (principle of tolerance or liberalism).

Rules on Hierarchy and Free Association

CC$_M$HFA1.0: Principle of hierarchical function within conversation (principle of social identity).

CC$_M$HFA2.0: Principle of free association outside conversation (principle of individual identity).

CC$_M$HFA3.0: Principle of spiritual Darwinism (principle of the ascent of the ethereal).

Rules on Education and Educability

CC$_M$EE1.0: Principle of formal education (principle of the induction of genius).

CC$_M$EE2.0: Principle of self-knowledge.

CC$_M$EE3.0: Principle of testing.

Rules on Ontology and Metaphysics

CC$_M$OM1.0: Principle of ontological satisfaction.

CC$_M$OM1.1: All conversational impulses are ontological.

CC$_M$OM1.2: Principle of double ontological reference.

CC$_M$OM2.0: Principle of emotional purification (principle of astral cleanliness).

CC$_M$OM3.0: Principle of meditation (principle of the meta-attitude).

CC$_M$OM4.0: Principle of physical law as such (principle of spatial manifestation).

CC$_M$OM5.0: The yoga of light.

CC$_M$OM6.0: Principle of universally acceptable causes (principle of the common cause).

CC$_M$OM7.0: Principle of metaphysical necessity.

CC$_M$OM8.0: Principle of as-if (principle of the acceptance of mystery).

NATURAL LAWS

Laws of Individuality

NLIn1.0: Genius is necessary for conversation.
NLIn2.0: Ineffability condition (first-order moments in the *logos* are absolutely unique).

Semantic Laws

NLSem1.0: Finiteness condition (Searlean taxonomy).
NLSem2.0: Law of conversational implicature.
NLSem3.0: Law of the social organism (law of absorption).

Moral Law

NLM: The categorical imperative (the moral law).

Psychological Laws

NLPsy1.0: Law of self-defense (law of comfort).
NLPsy2.0: Law of satisfaction (law of the cosmic centers).
NLPsy3.0: Law of antipathy.
NLPsy4.0: Law of free association.
NLPsy5.0: Law of sympathy (law of the free will).
NLPsy6.0: The imponderability of mood (law of disposition-ality).
NLPsy7.0: Purity and purification.
NLPsy8.0: Astral inversion.
NLPsy9.0: Law of love.
NLPsy10.0: Law of institutional reality (law of the mental filter).

Sociological Laws

NLSoc1.0: The subliminal civil war (the mechanism of degenerate collective intentionality).
NLSoc2.0: The cultural life.
NLSoc3.0: The economic life.
NLSoc4.0: The life of rights.

Physical Laws

NLPhy1.0: The conservation of energy (the great physical law).

NLPhy2.0: Law of the waking dream (continuity of consciousness).

NLPhy3.0: Law of spiritual discharge (capacitor principle).

NLPhy4.0: Principle of the physical field.

NLPhy5.0: Levitation.

NLPhy5.1: Up to down, down to up.

NLPhy5.2: Center to periphery, periphery to center.

NLPhy5.3: Spirals.

NLPhy6.0: Principle of reciprocal causality (everybody affects everybody else energetically just by being present).

NLPhy7.0: The spinal-mechanical principle (principle of the will).

BASIC TRANSCENDENTAL PRINCIPLES

Principles of Space and Time

CCST1.0: Principle of temporal circumscription (time condition).

CCST2.0: Principle of spatial awareness (space condition).

CCST2.1: Principle of spatial orientation.

Principles of Universal Representation

CCUniRep1.0: Principle of naming the content (principle of formal identification of the content).

CCUniRep1.1: Principle of preparation and preparedness (everyone has studied, exercised and rested).

CCUniRep1.2: Principle of universal prior knowledge of the content (everyone knows what is to be shared and is, in some sense, in possession of its text).

CCUniRep1.3: Principle of indifferent expression (it doesn't matter who says what needs to be said).

CCUniRep2.0: Principle of the mystical/magical text (what is to be shared is wonderful).

CCUniRep2.1: Principle of necessary concatenation (what is to be shared is stern and sublime).

CCUniRep3.0: In true conversation, everyone always knows exactly what was just said (principle of universal representation).

CCUniRep3.1: Everyone participating in a conversation can know exactly what was just said.

CCUniRep3.2: Everyone participating in a conversation should know exactly what was just said.

CCUniRep3.3: Principle of testing.

CCUniRep4.0: Principle of ontological nakedness (self-consciousness condition).

CCUniRep4.1: Principle of transparent motive (principle of contextual insensitivity).

CCUniRep4.2: Principle of idealistic motivation (principle of idealism).

CCUniRep4.3: Principle of motivation by love (love of the deed).

Principles of Expressibility and Causal Reference

CCExCR1.0: Principle of expressibility (principle of the conversational impulse).

CCExCR2.0: Principle of causal reference (principle of material efficiency).

Principles of Judgment

CCJ1.0: Principle of the judgment (principle of assertion).

CCJ1.1: Principle of judgmental circumspection (principle of reality invocation).

CCJ1.1.1: Principle of expectation (the social nature of rules).

CCJ1.1.1.1: Principle of external regulation (principle of heteronomy).

CCJ1.1.2: Principle of judgment as freedom.

Principles of the Directive

CCDir1.0: Principle of the directive.

CCDir1.1: Principle of universal direction.

CCDir1.2: The general will (what everybody wants, rationalized).

CCDir1.3: Principle of equal power (principle of the least intelligent).

Principles of Commissive, Expressive and Declaration

CCCED1.0: Principle of the commissive.
CCCED2.0: Principle of the expressive.
CCCED3.0: Principle of the declaration.

Principles of Engagement

CCEng1.0: Principle of engagement (principle of participation).
CCEng1.1: The limiting condition (if it is not possible to actualize a universal judgment with respect to some current content, conversation is not possible).
CCEng1.2: The law of call-and-response (the law of dialog).

Principles of Self-Regulation

CCSR1.0: Principle of self-regulation (principle of autonomy).
CCSR1.1: Principle of responsible control (principle of responsibility).
CCSR1.2: Principle of autonomy in conversational content.
CCSR1.3: Principle of self-knowledge (principle of self-consciousness).

Principles of Non-Sequitur

CCNS1.0: Principle of non-sequitur.
CCNS1.1: An individual who disputes a proposition or norm not under discussion must provide a reason for wanting to do so.

Principles of Logic

CCLog1.0: Principle of logic.
CCLog1.1: Principle of logical intelligibility.
CCLog1.2: Principle of logical notation.
CCLog1.3: Principle of logical proof.

CCLog1.4: No speaker may contradict himself (herself).

CCLog1.5: Every speaker who applies predicate F to object A must be prepared to apply F to all other objects resembling A in all relevant respects.

CCLog1.6: Different speakers may not use the same expression with different meanings.

CCLog1.7: Principle of reasonableness (no conversation is about nonsense).

CCLog1.8: Principle of good faith (no conversation is grounded on bad faith).

CCLog2.0: Principle of extensionality.

CCLog2.0: Basic conversational algorithm.

Principles of Truth

CCTr1.0: Only true judgments are allowed in conversation (principle of truth).

CCTr1.1: Every speaker may assert only what he (she) really believes (sincerity condition).

CCTr2.0: Truth is universal satisfaction (principle of pragmatism).

CCTr2.0: Principle of *logos* principle of the spirit of truth).

Principles of Freedom

CCFr1.0: In conversation, everyone is always free to say whatever he (she) wants to say (principle of freedom).

CCFr1.1: Everyone with the competence to speak and act is allowed to take part in a discourse.

CCFr1.2a: Everyone is allowed to question any assertion whatever.

CCFr1.2b: Everyone is allowed to introduce any assertion whatever into the discourse.

CCFr1.2c: Everyone is allowed to express his (her) attitudes, desires and needs.

CCFr1.3: No speaker may be prevented, by internal or external coercion, from exercising his (her) rights as represented in CCFr1.1 and CCFr1.2.

Divinity Principles

CCDiv1.0: Divinity principle (principle of authentic collective intentionality).

CCDiv1.1: Principle of the City of God (principle of divine cosmic evolution).

CCDiv1.2: Principle of cosmic competition (principle of culture and counter-culture).

Principles of Spiritual Initiation

CCSIn1.0: Principle of continuity.

CCSIn1.1: Principle of alchemy.

CCSIn1.2: Principle of silent work (seed principle).

CCSIn2.0: Principle of spiritual initiation (real conversation aims at spiritual initiation).

CCSIn2.1: Principle of equanimity (sit still and stay relaxed).

CCSIn2.2: Principle of positivity.

CCSIn2.3: Principle of open-mindedness.

CCSIn3.0: Principle of inspiration.

CCSIn3.1: Principle of the super-effort (principle of pure intentionality).

CCSIn4.0: Principle of the imagination (principle of fantasy).

CCSIn5.0: The exercise of thinking.

CCSIn6.0: The exercise of willing (principle of strength in the will).

CCSIn7.0: Principle of sacrifice.

CCSIn7.1: Principle of total sacrifice (sacrifice of the conversation).

Anthroposophical Principles

CCAn1.0: Principle of anthroposophical teleology (principle of Hegel's dialectic).

CCAn1.1: The anthroposophical principle (principle of the spiritual intellect).

Principles of Art and Self-Consciousness

CCArtSC1.0: The principle of self-consciousness (the principle of conversation as art).

CCArtSC1.1: The principle of conversational intentionality.

CCArtSC2.0: Principle of good posture (self-consciousness is basically posture).

CCArtSC3.0: The basic conversational cycle.

CCArtSC4.0: The idea of the simulacrum.

Principles of Meaning

CCMn1.0: The transcendental function of meaning (the condition on the possibility of *qualia*).

CCMn1.1: Principle of reproduction.

CCMn1.2: Principle of reproducibility.

CCMn1.2.1: Principle of indifferent reproducibility.

CCMn2.0: Principle of ideal mental contents (intellectual condition).

Principles of Social Pathology

CCSP1.0: Principle of selflessness.

CCSP2.0: Principle of social pathology.

CCSP2.1: Principle of tolerance.

CCSP2.2: The right of the anti-social.

CCSP2.3: The Social Duty Cluster.

CCSP3.0: Principle of contractual enumeration (principle of hashing out).

Principles of Love

CCLov1.0 Principle of sober love (principle of realism in love).

CCLov2.0: Principle of the etheric child (the reversal of the orgasm).

The Fundamental Social Law

> FSL: In a community of human beings working together, both the individual and the community as a whole are enriched and made better off the more the individual's needs are met directly by the activity of other people, and the less the individual's own activity benefits himself (herself) directly.

HYPOTHESES

Physical Hypotheses

HypPhy1.0: Hypothesis on physical law.

HypPhy2.0: Hypothesis of functional universality (theory of the good will as physical law).

HypPhy2.1: Hypothesis on physical space.

HypPhy3.0: The theory of the cosmic origins.

HypPhy4.0: Hypothesis on materiality (thought is sufficient for matter).

HypPhy4.1: Hypothesis on bliss (bliss is wave harmonics).

HypPhy4.2: The theory of wave functions (the physics of concepts).

HypPhy5.0: Theory of the fourth dimension.

Sociological Hypotheses

HypSoc1.0: Idea of reciprocal satisfaction (theory of the semantic cytoplasm).

HypSoc2.0: Theory of God's Program.

HypSoc2.1: Hypothesis on future earth evolution.

HypSoc2.2: Idea of cosmic construction.

HypSoc3.0: Hypothesis on the conversational index (the theory of conversation).

HypSoc3.1: Hypothesis on cosmic logic (the theory of conversation is cosmic).

Psychological Hypotheses

HypPsy1.0: Hypothesis on identical mental content.

HypPsy2.0: Hypothesis on projective geometry (theory of the ideal forms).

HypPsy2.1: Principle of the self.

HypPsy3.0: The theory of magic and the structure of magic.

HypPsy4.0: Hypothesis on the random generator.

HypPsy5.0: Hypothesis on causal self-reference (the theory of the sympathetic will).

HypPsy6.0: Hypothesis on inner sound.

HypPsy7.0: The presupposition of love (the foundation of psychological meaning).

HypPsy8.0: Hypothesis on the schematism.

HypPsy9.0: Hypothesis on the blood.

HypPsy9.1: Blood circulation is specifically restricted by mental contents.

Appendix C

PRIVATE PROPERTY

SOCRATES: And this agrees with the other principle, that the guardians are not to have houses or lands or any other property; that their pay is to be their food, which they receive from the other citizens; and they are to have no private expenses.

GLAUCON: Right.

Socrates: Both the community of property and the community of families will make them more truly guardians. They will not tear the City to pieces by differing about "mine" and "not mine." No man will drag any acquisition which he has made into a separate house of his own, where he has a separate wife and children and private pleasures and pains. Rather, all will be affected by the same pleasures and pains because they are all of one opinion about what is near and dear to them, and therefore they will tend toward a common end.

GLAUCON: Certainly.

SOCRATES: And I hardly need mention the little meannesses of which they will be rid, for they are beneath notice, such as for example the flattery of the rich by the poor, and the pains and pangs which men experience in bringing up a family, in finding money to buy necessities for the household, or borrowing and then repudiating, of getting how they can, of giving money into the hands of women and slaves to keep. The many evils of so many kinds which people suffer in this way are mean enough and obvious enough, and not worth speaking of.

GLAUCON: Yes, a man has no need of eyes in order to perceive that.

—PLATO, *The Republic*

The young man saith to him: All these commandments I have kept from my youth; what is yet wanting to me?

Jesus saith to him: If thou wilt be perfect, go sell what thou hast, and give to the poor, and so shalt have treasure in heaven: and come follow me.

And when the young man had heard this word, he went away sad: for he had great possessions.

—MATTHEW 19:20–22

The first person who having enclosed a plot of land took it into his head to say, "This is mine," and found people simple enough to believe him, was the true founder of modern society. What crimes, wars, murders, what miseries and horrors would the human race have been spared had someone pulled up the stakes or filled in the ditch and cried out to his fellow men, "Do not listen to this imposter. You are lost if you forget that the fruits of the earth belong to all and the earth to no one."

—JEAN-JACQUES ROUSSEAU, *Discourse on Inequality*

In the very centers of our civilization today are want and suffering enough to make sick at heart whoever does not close his eyes and steel his nerves. Dare we turn to the Creator and ask him to relieve it? Supposing the prayer were heard, and at the behest with which the universe sprang into being there should glow in the sun a greater power; new virtue fill the air; fresh vigor the soil; that for every blade of grass that now grows two should spring up, and the seed that now increases fifty-fold should increase a hundredfold! Would poverty be abated or want relieved? Manifestly no! Whatever benefit would accrue would be but temporary. The new powers streaming through the material universe could be utilized only through land. And land, being private property, the classes what now monopolize the bounty of the Creator would monopolize all the new bounty. Landowners would alone be benefited. Rents would increase, but wages would still tend to the starvation point!

—HENRY GEORGE, *Progress and Poverty*, 1879

In a community of human beings working together, both the individual and the community as a whole are enriched and made better off the more the individual's needs are met directly by the activity of other people, and the less the individual's own activity benefits himself (herself) directly.

—Rudolf Steiner, *The Fundamental Social Law*, 1905

Imagine no possessions,
I wonder if you can,
No need for greed or hunger,
A brotherhood of man,
Imagine all the people
Sharing all the world...

You may say I'm a dreamer,
but I'm not the only one,
I hope some day you'll join us,
And the world will live as one

—John Lennon, 1980

GLOSSARY

a priori: Latin, literally, *from the former.* Formed or conceived before starting. A rule or condition that sets initial conditions of a system, such as the conscious mind.

algorithm: From Arabic *al-khuwArizmi,* from *al-KhwArizmI fl A.D.* 825 Arabian mathematician. A step-by-step procedure for solving a problem or accomplishing some end especially by a computer.

Anthroposophy: A path of knowledge aiming to guide the spiritual element in the human being to the spiritual in the universe.

Aristotle's ratio: Rebelling from the revolutionary purity of his Master's ideas about government and human nature, Aristotle sought to bring matters down to earth by emphasizing a mean in all, or at least in most types of conduct. Take a point somewhere between timidity and recklessness and you get the true virtue of courage. For Aristotle, life on earth is a matter of discovering this mean. Phi, the so-called Golden Ratio, with its wonderful numerical properties, is a good candidate to be just this mean.

artificial life: A field of scientific study that seeks to model living biological systems through complex algorithms.

astral body: From Latin *astrum* star. The human soul.

astral world: From Latin *astrum star.* The soul world, including the souls of minerals, plants, animals and human beings.

autonomy: From Greek, self law. The quality or state of being self-governing

bhakti yoga: Sanskrit, literally, *portion.* Devotion to a deity constituting a way to salvation in Hinduism.

biologism: a modern materialist doctrine asserting all features of human consciousness to have a biological realization.

bivalence: From Latin, two powers. Having two possible values.

categorical analysis: An analysis reducing some complex phenomenon to a set of mutually exclusive categories. Biological taxonomy is a categorical analysis of life on earth.

categorical imperative: An imperative that commands without alternative.

clairvoyance: The power or faculty of discerning objects not present to the senses.

constitutive rules: Rules that constitute a formal game. Chess is nothing more and nothing less than the rules that govern the possible movements of the pieces.

conversational reproduction: The act of reproducing the motivation of some conversational action.

cosmos: The order underlying everything that exists.

counterspace: Negative or extra-dimensional space.

cultism: From Latin *cultus* care, adoration, from *colere* to cultivate. A usually small group of people characterized by devotion to a person, idea or system of practice.

cyborg: Cyber organism. A living body substantially replaced by intelligent mechanical or electro-mechanical components.

democracy: from Greek *dEmokratia,* from *dEmos* + *-kratia* –cracy. Government by the people.

deontic power: Greek *deont-, deon.* That which is obligatory, from neuter of present participle of *dein* to lack, be needful. Power of or relating to moral obligation.

deontology: The theory or study of moral obligation.

dianoia: Greek, literally, intellect.

ego: Latin, literally, *I.* The self, especially as contrasted with another self or the world.

epistemology: Greek *epistEmE* knowledge, from *epistanai* to understand, know, from *epi-* + *histanai* to cause to stand. The study or theory of the nature and grounds of knowledge especially with reference to its limits and validity.

etheric body: From Greek *aithEr,* from *aithein* to ignite, blaze. The rarefied element formerly believed to fill the upper regions of space. The upper regions of space: heaven. The spiritual body composed of the element giving rise to these conceptions.

etheric child: An alchemical product of concentrated spiritual activity.

etheric seed: An alchemical precursor produced by spiritual concentration.

etheric world: The world in its etheric aspect.

existential quantifier: The sign denoting a logical fiat by which of all imaginable possibilities it is asserted that at least one of these has a certain property.

extensionality: The property of objectivity. Transparency of reference. Treatable by logic.

fascism: Italian *fascismo,* from *fascio* bundle, fasces, group, from Latin *fascis* bundle & *fasces* fasces. A tendency toward or actual exercise of strong autocratic or dictatorial control.

first order logic: The logic of the terms AND, OR, NOT, IF … THEN, SOME, ALL.

free association: Social grouping according to instinctive attraction and aversion.

golden mean: The ratio of two members, whereby the magnitude of the second to the first equals the magnitude of the first to the sum of the first and the second. The ratio is 1.618….

Hegel's dialectic: The conversation of reason with itself, beginning with the concept of Being, and proceeding by negating each result, until all possible concepts are systematically understood and organized.

heteronomy: Subjection to something else.

ida: From yoga. The left or white channel of the etheric body, associated with the moon, spiraling up through the brain and terminating in the third eye.

ideal mental content: A mental content that produces complete satisfaction and stops the progression of association.

idealism: The theory that ultimate reality lies in a realm transcending phenomena.

illocutionary act: The performance of an act in saying something.

imagination: The material precursor to clairvoyance.

inner sense: Time.

intellect: Imagination trained on the sense world.

intension: The meaning of a context-laden term. Trying to get a framework of truth conditions to determine intensions is the objective of a Tarski-style intensional semantics.

intensionality: Opacity of reference. In "The sheriff believes Mr. Howard is an honest man," where "Mr. Howard" refers to Jesse James, the sentence itself doesn't allow us to decide whether it is true or false. Its truth or falsity must be referred to a circumstance wherein a contingent set of evaluative standards are applied. Intensional attitudes and expressions work against the possibility of pure conversation.

intersection: The propositions in common between the references of the current conversational content and the references of the conversational context developed to that point.

intuition: Perception.

Judeo-Christianity: The unique world historical moral tradition in which the monotheistic experience of a peculiar Semitic tribe is repudiated and remade by one of its exemplars for the sake of all humanity, with very difficult consequences and enormous worldly achievement for those who retain their identity.

karma: Sanskrit *karma* fate, work. The force generated by a person's actions held in Hinduism and Buddhism to perpetuate transmigration and in its ethical consequences to determine the nature of the person's next existence.

logos: Greek, speech, word, reason. The divine wisdom manifest in the creation, government, and redemption of the world and often identified with the second person of the Trinity. Reason that in ancient Greek philosophy is the controlling principle in the universe.

magic: Latin *magice,* from Greek *magikE,* feminine of *magikos*, from *magos* magus, sorcerer, of Iranian origin; akin to Old Persian *magus* sorcerer. The art of applying natural causes to produce surprising effects.

materialism: The theory that physical matter is the only or fundamental reality and that all being and processes and phenomena can be explained as manifestations or results of matter.

metaphysics: Medieval Latin *Metaphysica,* title of Aristotle's treatise on the subject, from Greek *(ta) meta (ta) physika,* literally, the (works) after the physical (works); from its position in his collected works. The division of philosophy that is concerned with the fundamental nature of reality and being and that includes ontology, cosmology, and often epistemology.

mereology: The study of part-whole and part-part relationships.

neurolinguistic programming: The study of the structure of subjective experience, with and emphasis on states of consciousness. Long in need of an effective moral compass, NLP may finally arrive as the essential and overarching framework of human communication.

normative: Latin *norma,* literally, carpenter's square. Conforming to a pre-conceived notion of how something should be.

ontology: New Latin *ontologia,* from *ont-* + *-logia* – ogy. A branch of metaphysics concerned with the nature and relations of being.

pingala: From yoga. The right or red channel of the etheric body, associated with the sun, spiraling into the brain and terminating in the third eye.

positivism: The doctrine that only real data should be taken into an account of metaphysics.

preterlogic: Logic applied to categories that do not constitute normal experience.

projective geometry: See synthetic geometry.

proposition: Something offered for consideration or acceptance. A proposal.

psychedelic: From *psych-* + Greek *dEloun* to show, from *dElos* evident; akin to Sanskrit *dIdeti* it shines, Latin *dies* day. Akin to deity. Showing the mind.

racism: A belief that racial differences produce an inherent and overall superiority of a particular race. Not to be confused with the fact of racial differences.

rationality: The capacity to apply logic to experience.

reason: The power of comprehending, inferring, or thinking in orderly rational ways.

res cogitans: A thinking thing; a soul. From Cartesian ontology, which divided existence into physical substances and mental substances.

sado-masochism: The derivation of pleasure from the infliction of physical or mental pain either on others or on oneself, often in a sexual context.

schema: Greek *schEmat-*, *schEma*. A diagrammatic presentation. An outline.

schemata: Plural of schema.

schematism: The disposition of constituents in a pattern or according to a schema. Design. *Also*: a particular systematic disposition of parts.

self-regulation: Effecting changes in oneself in response to feedback.

semantics: The study or theory of meanings.

simulacrum: Middle English, from Latin, from *simulare*. Image. Representation. Artificial world.

social contract: An actual or hypothetical agreement among individuals forming an organized society or between the community and the ruler that defines and limits the rights and duties of each.

social organism: A living entity of social constitution. A beehive, anthill or school of fish.

Socratic dialectic: A form of philosophical conversation departing from a controversial thesis, developing a well-formed antithesis and progressing to a synthesis, as the truths pertaining to each are retained.

spiritual intellect: A faculty of beholding supersensible order in sense phenomena.

state of nature: Every man for himself.

sushmna: From yoga. The central channel of the etheric body, containing the major chakras or dantiens, and terminating outside the crown of the etheric body.

synthetic: Being a proposition whose truth extends beyond the meaning of the words it contains, e.g. "The ocean contains many fish."

synthetic geometry: A branch of geometry that deals with the properties of configurations that are unaltered by projection.

transcendental: Of or relating to experience as determined by the mind's makeup. A condition on something's possibility.

Turing machine: An automaton which moves along a linear strip of data and performs certain actions according its state, which depends upon the data it has 'seen,' and the datum symbol that it is viewing.

Turing universality: A property of certain recursive functions in certain neural networks and other game-like schemata. Computability.

union: The total of all propositions under consideration.

universal quantifier: The sign denoting a logical fiat by which of all imaginable possibilities it is asserted that all of these has a certain property.

FURTHER READING & BIBLIOGRAPHY

Aurobindo, *Essays on the Gita,* Twin Lakes WI: Lotus Light Publications, 1995.

Crowley, Aleister. *Little Essays Toward Truth.* Las Vegas: New Falcon Publications, 1991.

Grof, Stanislav. *Psychology of the Future: Lessons from Modern Consciousness Research.* Albany, NY: SUNY Press, 2000.

Kaufmann, Walter. *Hegel: Texts and Commentary.* Notre Dame, IN: University of Notre Dame Press, 1977.

Hume, David. *An Enquiry Concerning Human Understanding.* Oxford: Clarendon Press, 1992.

Jung, Carl G. *Memories, Dreams, Reflections.* Aniela Jaffe, ed. New York: Vintage Books, 1973.

Kant, Immanuel. *Foundation of the Metaphysics of Morals.* New York: MacMillan. 1990.

———. *Prolegomena to Any Future Metaphysics.* Paul Carus, trans. Indianapolis, IN: Hackett Publishing, 1977.

Kripke, Saul A. *Naming and Necessity.* Cambridge: Harvard University Press, 1980.

———. *Wittgenstein on Rules and Private Language.* Cambridge, MA: Harvard University Press, 1982.

Locke, John. *Second Treatise of Government.* C.B. Macpherson, ed. Indianapolis, IN: Hackett Publishing, 1984.

Ouspensky, Peter D. *Tertium Organum: A Key to the Enigmas of the World.* New York: Vintage Books, 1970.

Regardie, Israel. The Tree of Life: A Study in Magic. York Beach, ME: Samuel Wieser, 1989.

Rousseau, Jean-Jacques. *The Social Contract.* Maurice Cranston, trans. New York: Penguin Classics, 1980.

Russell, Bertrand. "On Denoting." *Mind,* 14 (1905), pp 479–493.

Searle, John R. "A Taxonomy of Illocutionary Acts." In *Expression and Meaning.* New York: Cambridge University Press, 1979.

———. *Intentionality: An Essay in the Philosophy of Mind.* New York: Cambridge University Press, 1983.

———. *The Construction of Social Reality.* New York: The Free Press, 1995.

Steiner, Rudolf. *How to Know Higher Worlds: A Modern Path of Initiation*. Great Barrington, MA: Steinerbooks, 1994.

Vivekananda. *Meditation and Its Methods*. Hollywood, CA: Vedanta Press, 1978.

Index of Names